Jordan's
Palestinian Challenge,
1948–1983

Studies in International Politics

Leonard Davis Institute for International Relations,
The Hebrew University, Jerusalem

Jordan's Palestinian Challenge, 1948–1983:
A Political History
Clinton Bailey

Two-thirds of all Palestinians are Jordanian citizens living on the East and West Banks; a sizable number also reside and work in various parts of the Arabian Peninsula. With the questions of ultimate sovereignty over the West Bank and the Gaza Strip attracting much international attention since Israel's occupation of these areas in 1967, the solution to the Palestinian question is often seen as entirely dependent on Palestinian relations with Israel, despite the fact that only one-third of the Palestinians live in the occupied territories. In contrast, Palestinian relations with the Arab states, including Jordan, are generally portrayed as a sideshow to the main theater of conflict. This book examines the thirty-five-year struggle between the Hashimite monarchy and the forces of Palestinian nationalism over the future identity, and perhaps location, of those two-thirds of the Palestinian people who have been Jordanian subjects since 1948. Dr. Bailey bases his study on "open" sources: reports appearing in the Arab, Israeli, and world press, in addition to academic studies and published memoirs of persons involved in the events described, providing an accurate portrayal of the significant developments in Jordan's Palestinian challenge over the past thirty-five years.

Clinton Bailey was educated at Dartmouth College, The Hebrew University in Jerusalem, and Columbia University. Since 1973 he has taught in the Department of Middle East and African History at Tel Aviv University. His articles have appeared in leading academic journals dealing with the Middle East. He is also known for his studies of bedouin culture.

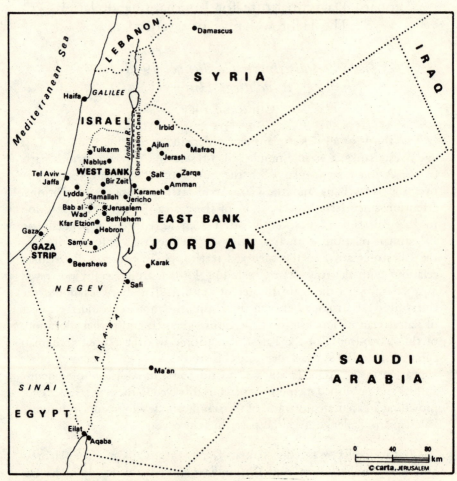

Jordan and Its Neighbors, 1983.

STUDIES IN INTERNATIONAL POLITICS
LEONARD DAVIS INSTITUTE FOR INTERNATIONAL RELATIONS
THE HEBREW UNIVERSITY, JERUSALEM

Jordan's Palestinian Challenge, 1948–1983: A Political History

Clinton Bailey

Westview Press • Boulder and London

*Studies in International Politics, The Leonard Davis Institute for
International Relations, The Hebrew University, Jerusalem*

Copyright © 1984 by Westview Press, Inc.

Published .in 1984 in the United States of America by Westview Press, Inc., 5500 Central
Avenue, Boulder, Colorado 80301; Frederick A. Praeger, Publisher

Library of Congress Cataloging in Publication Data
Bailey, Clinton.
    Jordan's Palestinian challenge, 1948–1983.
    (Studies in international politics / Leonard Davis
Institute for International Relations, The Hebrew
University, Jerusalem)
    Includes bibliographical references and index.
    1. Palestinian Arabs—Jordan—Politics and government.
2. Jordan—Politics and government. 3. Fedayeen.
I. Title. II. Series: Studies in international politics
(Boulder, Colo.)
DS153.55.P34B34 1984   956.95′0049275694   84-5161
ISBN 0-8133-0047-9

Printed and bound in the United States of America
10   9   8   7   6   5   4   3

FOR MAYA
whose faith and generosity,
patience and attentions
throughout the many years
made this first book possible

Contents

Preface

Two-thirds of all Palestinians are Jordanian citizens. They live in what is known as the East Bank and the West Bank; a sizable number also reside and work in various parts of the Arabian Peninsula. Should Jordan eventually also assume responsibility for the inhabitants of the Gaza Strip, 75 percent of all Palestinians will be Jordanian. As the question of ultimate sovereignty over the West Bank and the Gaza Strip has attracted much international attention since Israel's occupation of these areas in 1967, the solution to the Palestinian question is often seen as entirely dependent on Palestinian relations with Israel—this despite the fact that only one-third of the Palestinians live in the occupied territories. By contrast, Palestinian relations with the Arab states, Jordan included, are generally portrayed, if at all, as a sideshow to the main theater of conflict.

The present study attempts to portray the thirty-five-year struggle between the Hashimite monarchy and the forces of Palestinian nationalism over the future identity, and perhaps location, of those two-thirds of the Palestinian people who have been Jordanian subjects since 1948. Indeed, this is the struggle that will determine the ultimate destiny of the Palestinians as a people.

The analysis in this study is based almost entirely on "open" sources: primarily on reports appearing in the Arab, Israeli, and world press, in addition to academic studies, published memoirs of people involved in the events described, and two or three journalistic accounts. To compensate for the limitations of my sources, I have applied to this study eighteen years of observation that began with a Ph.D. thesis and continued with a close scrutiny of information that appeared in the media, as well as many conversations held with people involved in the subject, either personally or academically. I feel that the study is an accurate portrayal of the significant developments in Jordan's Palestinian challenge over the past thirty-five years.

This book would not have been written without the encouragement of two people. First and foremost is my spiritual father, Noah Jacobs, the philosopher and translator who, by example, taught me the meaning of integrity. He also taught me how to retain a sense of humor, even when dealing with the academic world. The second, Professor Uriel Dann, the historian, found value in my early perceptions of Jordanian politics and urged me to develop them. To both men my gratitude is herewith expressed.

The reader will note that (1) most Arabic names appearing in the text are transliterated as close to the Latin script equivalent as is possible without the use of many diacritical marks, which were deemed unnecessary for the Arabic reader and cumbersome for the non-Arabic reader; (2) a few names appear as they are commonly written in the U.S. press, such as Hussein (for Husayn), Assad (for Asad), and Gamal Abdul Nasser (for Jamal Abd al-Nasir); and (3) an apostrophe separating the letters of a word is to be understood as a glottal stop representing either the Arabic *alif* or the *ayin*.

Clinton Bailey
Jerusalem

INTRODUCTION

The Hashimite-Palestinian Struggle

On November 29, 1947, the General Assembly of the United Nations decided to partition British-mandated Palestine[1] and to create in its place two states, one Arab and the other Jewish. Two days later the Palestinian Arabs, in an effort to block the implementation of the UN resolution, began a civil war against the Jewish population by attacking intercity communications, outlying settlements, and public institutions.[2] Four months later, in April 1948, the Palestinian Jews counterattacked, and in the ensuing clashes the Palestinian Arab position collapsed. As a result, the leaders of five Arab states decided to send their armies into Palestine, each impelled by a variety of interests.[3]

One of these leaders was King Abdallah ibn al-Hussein al-Hashimi, who, in 1922, had come from Arabia to Transjordan, where he set up a state. Abdallah, believing his desert kingdom to be insufficient and convinced that his descent from the Prophet of Islam entitled him to

---

[1]That is, the area west of the Jordan River and the Araba valley. The original area of mandated Palestine, entrusted to Great Britain by the League of Nations after World War I, also included the area east of the river that, in 1922, was given a special status as the Emirate of Transjordan and placed out of bounds for Jewish settlement.

[2]This campaign was described in detail by a Jordanian Army officer who helped organize it. See Abdallah al-Tall, *Karithat Filastin* (*The Calamity of Palestine*). Cairo, 1959, pp. 3–10, 19–22, 98–102.

[3]See Yaakov Shimoni, "The Arabs and the Approaching War with Israel: 1945–1948" (in Hebrew), *Ha-Mizrah He-Hadash* 12 (1962), pp. 189–211.

a more notable domain, was ambitious to expand it.[4] Over the years he also feared that the nationalists who would come to power in a Palestinian Arab state, if it ever came into being, might cast an eye eastward toward Transjordan and undermine his throne. The king was therefore pleased when the end of the Palestine War, in 1949, found his army in control of all east-central Palestine, including the venerated Muslim shrines in the eastern part of Jerusalem. In 1950 he formally annexed this area (hence called "the West Bank") to Transjordan ("the East Bank"), renaming his kingdom Jordan.[5] He duly granted citizenship to the 810,000 Palestinians who thereby came under his authority and who, by outnumbering his original Transjordanian subjects two to one, became the majority in Jordan's population.[6]

Whereas the kingdom of Transjordan had been a peaceful polity before 1948, with most of the population in favor of the monarchy, the kingdom of Jordan was to be characterized by unrest for at least twenty-three years. Until 1971 the Hashimite regime (Kings Abdallah and Hussein, their relatives, and the politicians who identified with them) had to struggle to maintain control of the country against Palestinian nationalists who felt that the new Palestinian majority should determine Jordan's policies, policies that they hoped would enhance the Palestinian cause.

Moreover, the political aspirations of the two contending camps were diametrically opposed. The primary aspiration of the Palestinian nationalists was to see Israel destroyed so that they, themselves, could establish an Arab government in the whole of Palestine and enable the Palestinian refugees to return to their former homes. To them, Jordan's strategic position along Israel's eastern border obliged it to play a central role in the realization of these aspirations. The extent to which Jordan

---

[4]King Abdallah's ambitions were expressed in his Greater Syria Project of 1943, which envisaged his dominion over Transjordan, Syria, Lebanon, and Palestine. See Israel Gershuni, "King Abdallah's Concept of a 'Greater Syria,'" in A. Sinai and A. Pollack (eds.), *The Hashemite Kingdom of Jordan and the West Bank: A Handbook.* New York, 1977, pp. 139–147.

[5]King Abdallah engineered the annexation in three stages. On October 1, 1948, Palestinian notables met in Amman and declared that there could be no Palestinian government until Palestine was liberated. On December 1, 1948, a larger assembly of notables, meeting in Jericho, called for the unification of the East and West Banks under King Abdallah and for Palestinians to become members of Jordan's parliament. On April 24, 1950, a new Parliament approved the union of the two banks.

[6]International Bank for Reconstruction and Development [hereafter IBRD], *The Economic Development of Jordan.* Baltimore, 1957, p. 3.

assumed that role would determine the degree to which the very survival of the Hashimite regime was justified in Palestinian eyes. The primary aspiration of the Hashimite regime, on the other hand, was simply to rule, and, in its eyes, the country's raison d'être on both banks of the Jordan was to provide the territorial basis for that rule.

These respective aspirations of ruling, on the one hand, and "regaining" Palestine, on the other, proved impossible to reconcile, for what was beneficial to the one was detrimental to the other. For example, in order to finance its rule, the regime was dependent on grants from Great Britain and the United States, the only two powers sufficiently interested in the independent existence of the Hashimite monarchy to subsidize it. The Palestinian nationalists, however, objected to this financial dependence, believing that it enabled the two powers to influence Jordan's foreign and defense policies. They felt, in particular, that dependence on the West impelled Jordan to acquiesce with respect to the question of Israel's existence and to maintain quiet along the Israel-Jordan border. To Palestinian nationalists, the continual harassment of Israel over this border was essential in keeping their cause alive.

Whether or not the regime had an obligation to the powers that subsidized it, Jordan indeed adopted a policy of minimum confrontation with Israel designed to ensure that its rule would not be shaken by Israeli reprisal raids or by occupation, as eventually happened in the West Bank in 1967. Moreover, because of these conflicting attitudes on border policy, the regime sought to ensure that Jordan's army (often called the Arab Legion) was loyal and free from pro-Palestinian nationalist sympathies. It therefore recruited its important combat units mainly from dependable East Bank sections of the population—particularly from the bedouin and Circassians.[7] Furthermore, to prevent the Palestinian majority from imposing their political aspirations on the country, the rulers limited Palestinian participation in the major national decisionmaking bodies, where Palestinians were never allowed to enjoy representation commensurate with their two-thirds' majority. In both houses of the Jordanian parliament, parity of representation between the East and West Banks was the basis for representation, whereas the West Bank was more populous until the mid-1960s, when elections were last held.[8] East Bankers have also outnumbered Palestinians in almost all of

---

[7]Clinton Bailey, "The Participation of the Palestinians in the Politics of Jordan." Ph.D. thesis, Columbia University, 1966, pp. 108–117.

[8]Ibid., pp. 117–124.

the fifty or so Jordanian cabinets since 1950, and the longest of the three cabinets in which Palestinians actually constituted a majority served less than four months.[9] Moreover, only four of Jordan's nineteen prime ministers have been Palestinians, serving terms of eight days, nine days, one month, and fifty-five days, respectively.[10]

In their struggle to control the political direction of Jordan, both sides have exhibited strengths and weaknesses. The regime has enjoyed the practical advantages of military power with which to coerce the Palestinian nationalists if they became otherwise uncontrollable, as well as the means to affect the average Palestinian's standard of living. The "weakness" of the Hashimite regime, on the other hand, has been its desire for recognition by its Palestinian subjects as a legitimate government, without which its rule would never be secure. It is this aspiration of the regime that has been the Palestinian nationalists' main source of strength, giving them the ability to restrain government policies. These policies were also restrained by the regime's desire not to appear to violate the inter-Arab consensus, which generally pronounced in support of Palestinian nationalist goals.

Until 1971 the prevailing pattern of regime-Palestinian relations was such that the Palestinian nationalist leadership would expose and publicize government policies considered detrimental to their cause—policies involving the curbing of armed infiltration into Israel, the maintenance of secret contacts with the Jewish state, or the adherence to Western political initiatives that sought to end the Arab-Israel conflict. The nationalist leaders would then organize Palestinian crowds to demonstrate, knowing that a protest demonstration equalled a declaration that the regime was not representing Palestinian aspirations and therefore was not legitimate. Fearful of leaving yet another scar on regime-Palestinian relations, the regime was always wary of situations that might provoke it to use force against Palestinians. Between 1950 and 1970, the regime thus withdrew many unpopular policies before they could strain these relations too far.

In order to further its dual aspirations of ruling and being considered legitimate, the Hashimite regime, from 1949 to 1971, pursued a policy

---

[9]The cabinets of Hussein Fakhri al-Khalidi (Apr. 15–24, 1957) and Wasfi al-Tall (Dec. 2, 1962 to Mar. 27, 1963; Dec. 22, 1966 to Mar. 4, 1967).

[10]Hussein Fakhri al-Khalidi (Apr. 15–24, 1957), General Muhammad Da'ud (Sept. 16–24, 1970), Ahmad Tuqan (Sept. 26 to Oct. 28, 1970), and Qasim al-Rimawi (Jul. 3 to Aug. 28, 1980). See Clinton Bailey, "Cabinet Formation in Jordan," in Sinai and Pollack, *Hashemite Kingdom,* pp. 102–113.

of moderate hostility toward Israel—moderate as a precaution against being destroyed by its western neighbor, but hostile as a precaution against being overthrown by the Palestinians. The history of the regime in this period may be seen primarily as a constant struggle to strike a balance between these tendencies, as the Hashimites and the Palestinian nationalists each looked forward to some decisively favorable turn of events. The nationalists, while constantly preoccupied with trying to prevent the regime from coming to terms with the existence of Israel, looked forward to a time when the regime would fall. The Hashimites, while trying to prevent the complete disaffection of the Palestinian population, looked forward to a time when these same Palestinians would have to accept their regime as the best they could get—and this would happen only after they realized that they would neither destroy Israel nor attain an independent state of their own.

After 1971, when the Palestine Liberation Organization (PLO) was expelled from the country, having operated in Jordan since 1967, certain changes took place in the Hashimite-Palestinian struggle. The regime, for its part, continued to anticipate that the Palestinians it had absorbed in 1948 would ultimately view Jordan as their homeland and the Hashimites as their legitimate rulers, whereas the Palestinians, especially in the East Bank, ceased to occupy themselves with antiregime activity. After twenty-three years of unrest, the Palestinians began to enjoy the stability and prosperity that characterized the Jordan of the 1970s and early 1980s.

Between 1971 and 1983, the Hashimites' struggle with the Palestinian nationalists was waged primarily with the PLO, which operated from Beirut—a struggle that while bitter, was diplomatic rather than violent. Ostensibly, this was a contest that would decide who would inherit the West Bank and the Gaza Strip when and if Israel relinquished them. For the Hashimites, however, the struggle concerned the East Bank as well; should a Palestinian state be established west of the Jordan River, the 1.2 million Palestinians who came to constitute the majority east of the river might be tempted to include Jordan as a part of it. To King Hussein and his regime, it was a struggle for life or death.

ONE

Jordan, 1948–1967

YEARS OF INSTABILITY, 1948–1961

During the thirteen years after it had annexed the West Bank, the monarchy in Jordan was constantly on the defensive, forever fighting for its life. This was a period of instability for the inexperienced and unconfident regime as it tried to contend with the bitterness of the defeated and displaced Palestinians, and with their hopes of replacing the monarchy with Nasserism. It was a period marked by frequent demonstrations and riots, as well as by the assassinations of King Abdallah (1951) and Prime Minister Hazza al-Majali (1960) and an attempted military coup d'état (1957).

The five years between the Palestine War, which ended in 1949, and the advent of Nasserism in 1954 were marked by the rise of a new Palestinian nationalist leadership that occupied itself with organizing a popular backing. Unlike the mufti of Jerusalem and his political associates of an older generation who had led the Palestinians to defeat and dispersion in 1948, the Palestinian leaders who emerged in the Jordanian context were young (in their twenties and thirties), Western educated, and modern in their thoughts on political organization and activity. Most of their political experience had been gained in the three years between the end of World War II and the outbreak of the Palestine War, when they were being groomed for future leadership by the veteran Palestinian politician, Musa al-Alami. Although their opportunity to lead the Palestinians in a Palestinian state was not realized by 1948, they were the only group available to provide effective nationalist leadership when they became subjects of the Hashimite kingdom of Jordan.[11] All the former Palestinian leaders had fled abroad with the mufti.

---

[11] For more detail on the following, see Bailey, *Participation*, pp. 125–203.

7

For the first three years (1949–1951), the new leaders collaborated closely. The main figures were those who had become influenced by the Ba'th party of Syria: Abdallah al-Rimawi of Ramallah, Kamal Nasir and Musa Nasir of Bir Zayt, and Bahjat Abu Gharbiyyah and Abdallah Na'was of Jerusalem. The similarity between Ba'thist ideas and those of their mentor, Musa al-Alami, concerning inter-Arab affairs, the need for reform in Arab society, and the role of the Arabs in international relations was striking.[12] In 1953, when the young Palestinian leadership split up into several distinct parties, these men formed the nucleus of a Jordanian Ba'th party.

Another group of young intellectuals, differentiated from the others by their origins in noted Palestinian families, joined together to form the National Socialist party, which had an extreme nationalist appeal but no social ideology. The leading figures in this group were Anwar and Rashad al-Khatib of Hebron and Hikmat al-Masri of Nablus. In order to compete with these latter on a personal and familial basis, other young notables—such as Qadri Tuqan and Abd al-Qadir al-Salih in Nablus and Rashad Maswadah in Hebron—formed the National Front party, which was distinctly leftist in orientation and tended to cooperate with the West Bank Communists. The Communists, who had already been organized during Mandate times, were led by Dr. Abd al-Majid Abu Hijlah of Nablus, Fa'iq al-Warad of Ramallah, and Dr. Ya'qub Ziya al-Din of Jerusalem. At the opposite end of the political spectrum, the Liberation party, a right-wing religious party, was founded by Taqi al-Din al-Nabhani of Jerusalem and Ahmad al-Da'ur of Tulkarm. Despite their breakup into separate parties, however, the new Palestinian nationalist leaders who emerged in Jordan revealed a high degree of cooperation in organizing political activities and of solidarity in coming to each other's defense when each group, in turn, came under pressure from the regime.

The new Palestinian leadership was ill-disposed toward the Jordanian regime from the very outset. During the Palestine War of 1948–1949, they were informed by the Jordanian governor of Jerusalem, Colonel Abdallah al-Tall, of King Abdallah's "treachery to the Palestine cause"— namely, his surrendering of the towns of Ramlah and Lydda, his aban-

---

[12]Compare Musa Alami, "The Lesson of Palestine," *Middle East Journal* 3(4), 1949, pp. 373–405, with "The Constitution of the Party of the Arab Ba'th," in Sylvia Haim, *Arab Nationalism: An Anthology*. Berkeley and Los Angeles, 1962, pp. 233–241.

donment of the Egyptian army trapped at Faluja, his cession to Israel of 400 square kilometers at the Rhodes Armistice Talks, and his personal meetings with Israeli leaders in order to discuss peace.[13] It quickly became axiomatic to the young nationalists that they must strive to overthrow the regime if they were ever to get Jordan to play its role, as they saw it, in rectifying the situation in Palestine.

The ultimate goal in the Palestinian strategy that evolved was to effect the amalgamation of Jordan into a unified Arab state—usually comprising Egypt and Syria and, sometimes, Iraq. In Arab unity lay the Palestinians' grand hope for overcoming Israel. It was a lesson the nationalist leaders had learned from Musa al-Alami, who wrote: "The Arabs are stronger than the Jews if they unite and cooperate. . . . If the Arab armies had had a unified command during the Palestine War, they would have been able to collect their forces and aim them at the heart of the enemy in a powerful decisive blow. . . . The Arabs will not be strong until they are united. . . . Unity means freedom and independence."[14]

If Jordan were going to join such a union, however, the regime had to be toppled. It was obvious that the king of Jordan would not willingly forgo his rule for the sake of having Jordan join an Arab union that he was not to rule. To topple the regime, however, was all but impossible as long as Britain continued to underwrite the regime's existence with economic and military aid. As that aid, in turn, was conditional upon Jordan's army being under British officers, these officers—most notably General John Bagot Glubb, known as Glubb Pasha, who was the commander of Jordan's Arab Legion—had to be dismissed.

The only one of these goals that the Palestinian nationalists actually accomplished—the dismissal of Glubb and the British officers—was not achieved until 1956. Of course, the nationalists had not been inactive before then; foremost among their previous accomplishments was their success in thwarting all Jordanian attempts to come to terms with Israel's

---

[13]See al-Tall, pp. 247–257, 344–346, 420–435, 458–459, 467–468, 528–529. The 400-square-kilometer area surrendered to Israel had been occupied by the Iraqi army since May 1948. Iraq, not wishing to sign an armistice agreement with Israel following hostilities, sought to withdraw its army from this and other areas it occupied and to turn them over to Jordan. Israel, claiming that Jordan had no right to these areas, conditioned its agreement on its own acquisition of a part of the territory that it considered of strategic importance. This arrangement was included in the Israel-Jordan armistice agreements signed at Rhodes.

[14]Alami, "Lesson of Palestine," p. 388.

existence and the other results of the Palestine War. Not only did they expose various attempts to negotiate an actual peace treaty—attempts that were then quickly terminated—but they also kept the government in a state of constant embarrassment for having signed the Rhodes Armistice Agreements with Israel. The agreements required the government to cede 400 square kilometers of Arab-held land in the "Little Triangle" to the Jewish state and to maintain quiet along the Jordan-Israel border.[15] Finally, the nationalist leadership succeeded in causing the Palestinian refugees to reject the idea of resettlement outside Israel.

The impeding of the regime's efforts to acquiesce to the Palestinian status quo was accomplished in several ways. The nationalists both publicized all government moves on the subject, either in the press or in parliamentary debates,[16] and organized public demonstrations and disorders. These activities, in turn, resulted in the politicization of the Palestinian population, which greatly benefited the nationalists' cause. They succeeded in inculcating the Palestinians with the conviction that the continuation of the Jordanian regime was the chief reason for the prolongation of the Palestinian misfortune. At the same time they established, as axiomatic, that the ultimate responsibility for the Palestinian condition lay in Jordan's British connection. The British-commanded Arab Legion, they pointed out, restrained Arab operations against the Israelis across the border, and, when the Palestinians did manage to strike, the army did not protect the Palestinian border villages from Israeli reprisals. The nationalists thus saw to it that every reprisal was followed by violent demonstrations and protests.

This politicization of the Palestinian people proved crucial to the nationalists in their tests of strength against the regime between 1954 and 1956. By then, the nationalists had developed an organization that they could wield effectively when greater opportunities for action arose, as happened in 1954. That was the year when Gamal Abdul Nasser came to power in Egypt and succeeded in negotiating the withdrawal of British forces from the Suez Canal Zone, thereby demonstrating his abilities as a leader who could attain what had previously been considered

---

[15]Excerpts from the text of the agreement appear in Sinai and Pollack, *Hashemite Kingdom*, pp. 341–342.

[16]While parliament was not sovereign in the kingdom of Jordan, it served as a forum where embarrassing situations could be created and government policies criticized. Similarly, while censorship of the press existed, it was not always strictly applied. On occasion, editors would risk punishment in order to expose policies they considered inimical to the Palestinian cause.

unattainable. Thus, when Arab unity—which the Palestinian nationalists considered a panacea—became a cornerstone of Nasser's foreign policy, Nasser became the Palestinians' natural ally. Similarly, as Nasser was interested in toppling British-backed Arab regimes, such as that in Jordan, the Palestinians became his natural allies.

Egyptian funds subsequently began to pour into the nationalists' coffers on the West Bank, together with directives for antiregime activity. At the same time, the Egyptians waged a vicious and intensive anti-Hashimite propaganda campaign over the radio, aimed at raising Palestinian hopes, on the one hand, and weakening the resolve of the regime and its supporters, on the other. Syria and Saudi Arabia, each separately at odds with the British over narrower issues, also produced funds for antimonarchist activities. It seemed as if the entire Arab world had turned against the inexperienced young King Hussein, who had ascended to the throne on May 2, 1953, at the age of eighteen.

The politicization of the Palestinians, focusing as it did on the role of Britain in the Palestinian misfortune, facilitated their recruitment in the campaign against Jordan's plans to join the British-sponsored Baghdad Pact in 1955. The Baghdad Pact, formed in February of that year, was a defense organization comprising Britain, Turkey, Iran, Pakistan, and Iraq. Arab nationalists everywhere, and in Egypt in particular, opposed the pact. Nasser not only viewed with disfavor the further entrenchment of British influence in the Middle East, which Britain's sponsorship of and membership in the pact was sure to afford, but he was also displeased with the increased prestige and power that membership in the pact would confer on Egypt's greatest traditional rival, Iraq.

From the outset, Egypt had waged an intensive campaign against Iraq's plans to join the pact, but had failed. Its efforts to prevent Syria from joining, however, were crowned with success;[17] now, strengthened by Nasser's ever-growing prestige, due to his weapons deal with the Soviet Union and his prominence at the Bandung Conference of Non-Aligned Nations in 1955, Egypt embarked on a campaign to keep Jordan out of the pact.

In December 1955, when Jordan was expected to reply to an invitation to join the pact, Nasser's campaign began in earnest. Attacks on the regime, broadcast from Egypt, Syria, and Saudi Arabia, branded adherence to the Baghdad Pact as treason to the Palestinian cause. Anwar al-Sadat, then a member of the Egyptian Revolutionary Command Council, was

---

[17]See Patrick Seale, *The Struggle for Syria*. London, 1965, pp. 197–199.

sent to Amman where he personally intimidated cabinet members, while over £60,000 ($144,000) were sent into the country to finance riots and disorders. The Egyptian success was overwhelming. Violent demonstrations broke out in Amman and in all the major towns of the West Bank. The French and Turkish consulates in Jerusalem were blown up, United Nations Relief and Works Agency (UNRWA) offices were destroyed, and even the experimental farm of Musa al-Alami, near Jericho, was destroyed. After three cabinets fell within twenty-three days, the regime backed down. It was not to join the Baghdad Pact.

Young King Hussein was bewildered and in despair. The British connection, upon which the survival of the monarchy had always depended, not only proved unable to help him now but might indeed have led to his removal from the throne. Without knowing exactly what results to expect, the king realized that he must sever Jordan's identification with England. Therefore, on the heels of the Baghdad Pact affair, when the victory-flushed nationalists began to demand the dismissal of the Legion's English officers, Hussein felt constrained to comply. On March 1, 1956, Glubb Pasha, who had spent twenty-six years in Jordan, left on twenty-four hours' notice. The first strategic goal of the Palestinian nationalists had finally been achieved, and control of the Legion fell into the hands of a group of young pro-Nasser officers led by Ali Abu Nuwwar, who, although an East Banker, had always been very sympathetic to the Palestinian cause.[18]

Events then moved quickly, in keeping with the Palestinian strategy. With the Arab Legion now in sympathetic hands, the nationalists demanded the dissolution of the existing Chamber of Deputies—namely, the lower house of Jordan's parliament, which had been packed with supporters of the regime—and called for free elections. These elections, held in June 1956, returned an overwhelming antiregime majority of representatives who formed a "national" government under the premiership of Sulayman al-Nabulsi, an antiregime politician from the East Bank town of Salt. Serving prominently in Nabulsi's cabinet were five members of his own National Socialist party, a member of the Ba'th

---

[18]Abu Nuwwar came under the influence of Col. Abdallah al-Tall during the Palestine War and the Rhodes armistice negotiations. He was "banished" to the post of military attaché in the Jordan embassy in Paris by Glubb Pasha. There, he escorted the young Hussein on the latter's visits to the French capital. In 1955, Hussein made Abu Nuwwar his aide-de-camp (ADC), from which position he not only counseled the dismissal of Glubb Pasha but also maneuvered himself into the post of chief of staff.

party (Abdallah al-Rimawi, as minister of state for foreign affairs), and a member of the extreme leftist National Front (Abd al-Qadir al-Salih).

One of Nabulsi's first acts was to abrogate the treaty with Great Britain under which that country had subsidized Jordan. In its stead an agreement was reached with Egypt, Saudi Arabia, and Syria, whereby they would provide the £12,500,000 ($30 million) per year that Britain had been paying. The Palestinian nationalists considered this an important achievement. If England had been able to dictate Jordanian policies in the past, these would now be determined by Arab nationalist subsidizers.

Other popular steps were taken in the direction of the much-coveted idea of Arab unity. In October 1956, Jordan signed an agreement providing for the unification of the Jordanian, Egyptian, and Syrian military commands in the event of a war with Israel. In March 1957, a further agreement was signed with Egypt and Syria. This was a cultural agreement providing for a unified curriculum for the schools of the three countries "in order to form an Arab generation believing in the Arab motherland." To many Palestinians, complete Arab unity seemed just around the corner.

In a last-ditch effort to check this march of events, King Hussein, reportedly encouraged by the United States,[19] confronted Nabulsi on his ostensible drift toward communism: Nabulsi had established diplomatic relations with the Soviet Union and had released convicted Communists from prison.[20] Two Communists had been elected to the Chamber of Deputies,[21] while another, considered a fellow-traveler, was included in the cabinet.[22] When the king raised objections, which Nabulsi duly ignored, Hussein dismissed his cabinet. At that moment, the nationalist officers who controlled Jordan's army feared that they might lose their newly acquired power and plotted to overthrow the king. On April 14, 1957, the commander of the Legion, Ali Abu Nuwwar, mobilized an armored regiment that he sent to Amman to encircle the palace, depose the king, and send him into exile in Cyprus. Informed in advance by various bedouin troops, however, King Hussein was able to rally

---

[19]Units of the U.S. Sixth Fleet were moved to the eastern Mediterranean, and the White House declared that it considered the "independence of Jordan" as vital.

[20]The Communist party was outlawed in Jordan under a law passed in 1953.

[21]Yaqub Ziya al-Din and Fa'iq al-Warad.

[22]Abd al-Qadir al-Salih, as minister of agriculture.

loyal units and crush the revolt.[23] Some rebel officers were arrested, while others fled from the country with Abu Nuwwar.

Arrest or flight was also the fate of the Palestinian nationalists who were implicated in the planning of the military coup and in the organization of widespread riots a few days later. Military administration was imposed throughout the country, and all antiregime activities were summarily dealt with. By the end of April, it was perfectly clear that the young King Hussein had completely turned the tables on the Palestinian antiregime forces. Their leadership was now either silenced, arrested, or in exile. Their organization no longer existed.

For the monarchy, the next three years were nonetheless fraught with tension. Beginning in February 1958, Egypt and Syria were unified in the United Arab Republic (UAR). The fact that the two Arab countries had dissolved their individual sovereignties and united created great excitement among Jordan's Palestinians and heightened their disaffection from the Hashimite regime. What right, they asked, did Jordan have to hold on to a separate national existence now that Egypt and Syria had forgone theirs? Their malaise was aggravated by the UAR in three ways. First, the UAR mounted the most intensive and abusive campaign to date against the regime, calling upon the Jordanian populace to rebel. Second, it attempted to demoralize the regime by sending terrorists from Syria into the country to undertake acts of sabotage and murder. Jordan was thus subjected to a spate of bomb-throwing, and attempts were made to blow up bridges, telegraph poles, airports, a governor's car, embassies, and the homes of officials. Army plots were organized as well. Finally, in the most successful antiregime operation, Prime Minister Hazza al-Majali was assassinated on August 29, 1960.

A further UAR attempt to estrange the Palestinians from the regime was its proposal at the Arab League, in March 1959, to establish a "Palestine Entity." The proposal called for the establishment of Palestinian representative bodies and a Palestinian army that would fight for the "reconquest" of Palestine. For the Hashimite regime this proposal represented a direct challenge not only to the sovereignty of Jordan over the West Bank but also to its hopes for uniting the Jordanian and Palestinian sections of the population under its rule. Its discomfort was eased only when the UAR itself dropped the plan because of the opposition

---

[23]King Hussein of Jordan, *Uneasy Lies the Head.* New York, 1962, pp. 169ff.

of other Arab states. Nevertheless, the very proposal did serve to enhance the credit that President Nasser already enjoyed among the Palestinians.[24]

The pressures exerted by the UAR on Jordan between 1958 and 1961, however, were to no avail. There was no Palestinian leadership and organization operating inside Jordan that could utilize the Egyptian and Syrian assistance in order to foment rebellion. Antiregime sentiment, without local leadership to activate and channel it, could not in itself be effective.

THE ENTRENCHMENT OF THE REGIME, 1961-1965

In September 1961 the UAR, the union between Egypt and Syria that had lasted for three and a half years, broke up. From a Jordanian point of view, this was a highly important development. Many Palestinians had been convinced that a union of Arab countries, forming a ring around Israel, would inevitably lead to the defeat and destruction of the Jewish state, and they had been incensed that Jordan would not join the union of the two major Arab states. What right did Jordan, with two-thirds of its population Palestinian, have to exist when it refused to comply with that majority's paramount aspirations and join an Arab union?

These sentiments lost their meaning, however, when the UAR broke up. One could no longer criticize King Hussein for not sacrificing Jordan's independence and sovereignty to the Palestinian cause, after Egypt and Syria had failed to do so. Despair as to the possibility of ever regaining Palestine began to grip the Palestinians. If Arab unity did not work, what would?

The full impact of this despair was felt, however, only a year and a half later. In March 1963, after successful revolutions had been engineered by the Ba'th party in Damascus and Baghdad, another possibility of Arab unity arose as discussions for a new union were held between the three strongest Arab states—Egypt, Syria, and Iraq. Once again the Palestinians were hopeful. On April 14, after the union had been proclaimed, the following statement appeared in *al Gumhuriyyah*, the Egyptian daily: "If there is any absolute and complete joy to Arabs in the establishment of a large, new and united state, it is the joy of the Palestinians. . . . The Palestinians see in the new state the beginning

---

[24]For more details, see Yitzhak Oron (ed.), *Middle East Record, 1960.* Tel Aviv, 1962, pp. 132-138.

of their salvation from the suffering, humiliation, dispersion and despair
with which they have been living for fifteen years. . . . Arab union is
the only path by which they will regain their natural existence."

When the talks for implementing the union were actually being held,
the enthusiasm of the Palestinian population in Jordan exploded, and
in May 1963, widespread rioting broke out for the first time since 1957.
Palestinian mobs demanded that Jordan join this tripartite union, and
they were so implacable that two successive cabinets were forced to
resign.

Then, in mid-May, the Egyptians suddenly announced that there would
be no union; agreement could not be reached and the talks were called
off. The Palestinians were stunned. "Which side was to blame?" they
asked. But when Cairo Radio broadcast the protocols of all the discussions
about the union, it became clear that all sides were to blame: Nasser,
the Syrians, and the Iraqis. The actual discussions revealed that the
respective parties were unwilling to subordinate their own parochial,
partisan interests and to act on behalf of the Palestinian, or Arab, cause.[25]

In the wake of this Palestinian disillusionment, the regime was no
longer under pressure to justify its existence. Shortly thereafter, Jordan
also ceased to be isolated in the Arab political arena and to be the sole
target of Arab indignation and incitement. The early 1960s witnessed
several conflicts between various other Arab countries, each conflict taking
priority over antipathy to Jordan. Initially, there were frictions between
Egypt and the government of Ma'mun Kuzbari that had taken Syria out
of the United Arab Republic. Then Egypt's relations with the Ba'th
regimes, which came to power in Syria and Iraq, became strained. By
late 1963, the Ba'th regimes had become antagonistic to each other. At
the same time, Egypt was at odds with Saudi Arabia over the war in
Yemen. At different times, too, Egypt and Syria attacked the "reactionary"
regimes of Saudi Arabia, Morocco, and Tunisia, as well as that of Jordan.
In the mid-1960s, hostility was also predominant in the relations between
the newly independent Maghrebian states because of border disputes
and the question of Mauretania's future.

With divisiveness in the Arab world clearly on the rise, the Palestinians
began to have second thoughts about their future. Perhaps they would
not regain Palestine for a long time. Moreover, since no benefit was to
be had from pinning their hopes on the enemies of Jordan, it might

---

[25]For a study of these talks, see Malcolm Kerr, *The Arab Cold War—1958–
1964* (Chatham House Essays: 10). London, 1965, pp. 55–126.

be wise to come to terms with the regime and build a future for themselves in the Hashimite kingdom. This tendency was particularly pronounced among the nationalist leaders who had devoted the previous fifteen or so years to opposing the regime. After 1961 they not only made their peace with the king but also agreed to serve him. For example, Anwar al-Khatib of the National Socialist party, who had been an Egyptian agent during the 1950s, was in 1964 considered to have become trustworthy enough to be sent to Egypt as Jordan's ambassador. His cousin, Rashad al-Khatib, who had been sentenced to a year's imprisonment in 1957 for inciting to riot, became the minister for national economy.

Three other leading opponents of the regime in the 1950s—Musa Nasir, a Ba'th sympathizer; Hana Atallah, a founder of the pro-Egyptian National Socialist party; and Qadri Tuqan, of the leftist National Front party—all served as foreign ministers in the 1960s. A party colleague of Tuqan, Abd al-Qadir al-Salih, became the minister of defense and minister of state for prime minister affairs. During this period, moreover, members of the Husayni and Anabtawi families—the most rabid of anti-Hashimites—were happy to receive ministerial positions. The list of oppositionists who joined the ranks of the regime could go on even further.

In addition to giving cabinet positions to former oppositionists, the regime also made special efforts to defer to Palestinian sensibilities. This was done, in part, by a judicious choice of cabinet ministers. For example, Prime Ministers Bahjat Talhuni and Wasfi al-Tall were chosen to head cabinets in the early 1960s, as both were popular with the Palestinians at the time. Too many memories of mistrust and suppression from the 1950s were associated with the traditional choices of prime minister—such as Ibrahim Hashim, Samir al-Rifa'i, and Sa'id al-Mufti—for these men to return to office. King Hussein also made liberal use of his right to grant amnesties in order to pardon persons accused of plotting against the government and even against the life of the king himself. Thus, several East Bank officers of the Legion, including such prominent plotters as Abdallah al-Tall, Ali Abu Nuwwar, and Ali al-Hiyari, were allowed to return to Jordan from exile on the condition that they not engage in politics. Abu Nuwwar was subsequently appointed Jordan's ambassador to France, whereas al-Hiyari, who had been Abu Nuwwar's chief accomplice in the plot to overthrow the king in 1957, was appointed chief of staff of the Legion in 1970. In addition, the veteran leader of all East Bank opposition to the regime, Subhi Abu Ghanimah, was allowed to return to Jordan from Syria where he had spent thirty years in exile. Indicative of the extent to which antiregime nationalists came to terms with the regime was Abu Ghanimah's return to Syria as Jordan's ambassador.

Although the degree to which the regime became acceptable to many Palestinians was largely determined by political factors, both internal and external, Jordan's improved economic condition also served as an incentive for them to envisage a future in that country. When King Abdallah first occupied the West Bank in 1948, Jordan's economy had more problems than promise. The population of the country immediately tripled, whereas the basic grain and livestock production of the West Bank was only one-third that of Transjordan.[26] Half the additional population, moreover, consisted of refugees who had to be supported by the state. Jordan had but a few domestic industries, all of them primitive. Even agriculture, which accounted for three-quarters of the gross national product (GNP), was unpredictable. Because of the uneven rainfall, agricultural production could fluctuate by over 90 percent annually. In 1959, because of drought, it was worth only £11,000,000 ($26.4 million); in 1961, a year of heavy rainfall, the value of the produce rose to £23,000,000 ($55.2 million).[27]

Under such circumstances, the question was not how the citizenry would thrive, but how the state would survive at all. The answer lay in Jordan's most important asset—its strategic position vital to the West. Since the establishment of the emirate of Transjordan in 1922, the British had paid for this asset with annual subsidies that rose from £60,000 ($144,000) to £12,500,000 ($30 million) by 1956 when the subsidy was canceled. Initially, the British interest lay in maintaining a friendly regime in what it considered a vital sphere of influence; later it lay in having a pro-West regime in the northeastern approaches to the oil-rich Arabian peninsula. In 1957 the United States took over the financial responsibility for the upkeep of the regime for the same reason, which was deemed sufficiently important to warrant a yearly outlay of over $55,000,000 (£23 million) by 1966.[28] These subsidies provided by the United Kingdom and the United States, in addition to the annual sum spent by UNRWA in Jordan ($13,000,000 [£5.4 million] in 1966), enabled this otherwise poor country to live on imports. The foreign

---

[26]IBRD (1957), p. 3.

[27]H. Talal, "Growth and Stability in the Jordan Economy," *Middle East Journal* 21(1), 1967, p. 99.

[28]See table in Sinai and Pollack, *Hashemite Kingdom,* pp. 170–171.

currency flow into Jordan not only covered its balance-of-payments' deficit but also left a sterling balance in the Hashimite kingdom's account.[29]

However, although the regime managed to survive economically on foreign aid, the acceptance of this aid proved, politically, to be a perennial weak spot in its efforts to appear legitimate. For example, in the early 1950s, the Palestinian nationalists exploited this weakness—that Jordan was not viable economically—in order to strengthen their demand that it amalgamate with another Arab state (preferably Egypt or Iraq) that was able to pay Jordan's way and would, they believed, also utilize Jordan in the Arab interest—in particular, in the effort to destroy Israel.

It took ten years for the regime to contend with this weak spot in its political status. It was Hazza al-Majali, appointed prime minister in 1959, who, in the face of an Iraqi proposal at the Arab League for the establishment of a political entity for the Palestinians in the West Bank, devised a policy of ruling the country on the basis of popular consensus rather than by armed force. In addition to the administrative reforms he initiated during his tenure of office, he introduced measures for building an economic infrastructure. His long-term hope was for a degree of economic independence for Jordan. In the short run, however, his economic measures sought to counter the argument of the regime's enemies that Jordan was an illegitimate state because its lack of viability enabled non-Arab powers to determine its policies.

The infrastructure developed in the six years preceding the Six-Day War of 1967 included the expansion of agricultural production, the development of natural resources such as phosphates and potash, the construction and improvement of roads, the expansion of Jordan's sole port at Aqaba, the encouragement of domestic industry, and, not least, the development of tourist facilities.[30] Chief among the development projects was the East Ghor Canal, which opened up new areas of land for agriculture on an irrigated and, hence, more dependable basis. When the canal was completed in 1964, 30,000 additional acres of irrigated land were added to the agricultural sector. In the same period an oil refinery was constructed at Zarqa, making Jordan independent of imports of refined oil products.

This activity of the early 1960s promised not only a brighter economy for the future but brought immediate rewards as well. For example,

---

[29]E. Kanovsky, "The Economic Aftermath of the Six-Day War, Part II," *Middle East Journal* 22(3), 1968, p. 288.

[30]The following information is taken from E. Kanovsky, *The Economy of Jordan.* Tel Aviv, 1976, pp. 3–17.

construction, as in the city of Amman, which had grown tenfold to 300,000 inhabitants between 1948 and 1966 (the result of the large-scale emigration of Palestinians from the West to East Bank), provided employment for thousands of workers. In the period between 1954 and 1966, Jordan could boast about an average annual growth of 8 percent in GNP, an increase higher than any of the neighboring non-oil-producing Arab states. After 1960 the average was actually higher; in 1960–1961, for example, it rose by 23 percent.

At the same time, prices remained stable and imported goods were accessible, so that middle-class Jordanians, at least, could enjoy the fruits of the expanding economy. Tourists were also visiting the country; in 1966 Jordan received 600,000 tourists who spent over $30 million (£12.5 million), an increase of 200 percent since 1960. Many hotels and other tourist facilities were built, but Jordanians on both the East and West Banks (primarily the West) profited from this growth in tourism. Indeed, it was difficult to deny that this benefit was due primarily to the initiative of the regime.

THE STRUGGLE WITH PALESTINIAN
NATIONALISM BEFORE THE SIX-DAY WAR

The assimilation of the Palestinians, which began in the early and mid-1960s, was largely a result of their disappointment over the failure of the major Arab states to unite. However, although significant in indicating that there were conditions under which Palestinians might settle for a non-Palestinian future, this acquiescence to the regime was not universal in 1966. Not all Palestinians were sufficiently in despair at the failure of Arab unity as to abandon the idea of "reconquering" the part of Palestine that was Israel. One refugee in particular, Yasir Arafat, had never believed in the concept that "Arab unity was the road to the liberation of Palestine." Indeed, he was convinced of the opposite— namely, that "the liberation of Palestine was the road to Arab unity."[31]

According to Arafat, the realization of Arab unity required the concession of so many vested interests that it could only take place in an apocalyptic atmosphere. The only event that could create such an atmosphere would be the liberation of Palestine. To Arafat's mind, the emergence of Israel was a wrong that, remaining unredressed, paralyzed

---

[31]Y. Harkabi, *Fedayeen Action and Arab Strategy* (Adelphi Papers, 53; the Institute for Strategic Studies). London, 1968, pp. 8–11.

every positive Arab political initiative, including unity. The path to the liberation of Palestine, as he understood it, was the mobilization and armed struggle of the Palestinians themselves. According to Arafat, it was important for the Palestinians to struggle by themselves, as such a struggle would free them from the patronage of the Arab states that invariably placed their own national interests above the Palestinian cause and desisted from the final confrontation with Israel. The Palestinian armed struggle, by contrast, would precipitate that confrontation despite the reluctance of the other Arabs. By goading the Israelis with guerrilla and terrorist operations, and by embarrassing the Arab states into action, the Palestinians themselves would bring about the much-anticipated clash.

Arafat's concept of Palestinian self-help and of a specific Palestinian identity posed a particular threat to the "Jordanian identity" that King Hussein hoped his Palestinian majority would eventually adopt. This was not, however, the first such threat. The first had occurred in March 1959, when Nasser proposed to the Arab League the establishment of a "Palestine Entity." Egypt's idea was that each Arab country should enable its Palestinians to establish popular representative organizations and that these should be merged into one main body and attached to the Arab League. The program also envisaged the formation of a Palestinian army to be organized in the host countries. Egypt put forward these proposals primarily to embarrass King Hussein, expecting that the king would find it difficult to rebuff openly Palestinian aspirations for independent action.

Another reason for raising the idea of Palestinian self-help and identity was to score a propaganda point over Egypt's traditional rival, Iraq; but Iraq, not to be outdone, made even more far-reaching counterproposals. Its ruler, General Abd al-Karim Qasim, called for the immediate establishment of a Palestinian republic in the West Bank and the Gaza Strip, to be headed by a provisional government. Iraq went further and actually set up Palestinian units in its army, which later formed the nucleus of the Palestine Liberation Army. To Jordan's relief, the Arab League never accepted the Palestine Entity plan because Egypt and Iraq kept vetoing each other's proposals at League meetings. Then, when the two rivals finally decided to "make peace" in late 1960, they shelved the controversial proposals indefinitely.

In September 1963, however, Egypt, at the Arab League, put forward another plan for independent Palestinian activity, the initiative once again emanating from the dictates of Egypt's own national interests. During the previous month, Israel had completed construction of its national water carrier, which was to convey water from the Sea of Galilee south to the Negev. Despite the repeated Egyptian threats over the preceding two years that Egypt would prevent its operation, Nasser, who was concurrently engaged in the Yemen War, was in no position to take action. His leadership in the Arab world was consequently jeopardized, much to the pleasure of the Arab Ba'th party regimes in Syria and Iraq, who were his bitter rivals for leadership.[32]

Thus, once again, Egypt sought to solve its problems with inter-Arab relations by exploiting the Palestine issue. To strengthen its reputation as the patron of the Palestinian cause against allegations that it was neglecting the cause by allowing Israel to irrigate and thus develop the Negev with the water from the Jordan River, Egypt proposed in 1963 the establishment of the Palestine Liberation Organization (PLO). The responsibility for organizing the PLO was put into the hands of Ahmad al-Shuqayri, an outspoken Palestinian who, until shortly before, had been the Saudi Arabian ambassador to the United Nations. Shuqayri's first important task was to hold individual talks with the heads of the Arab states and to canvass support for the project.[33]

As in 1959, Jordan was again vulnerable to the implications of Egypt's proposals. Shuqayri demanded that Jordan set up separate Palestinian military units in the West Bank with Palestinian officers, that Jordan arm all Palestinians living along the border with Israel, that the salaries of Palestinians be taxed for a special Palestine National Fund, and that various Palestinian administrative bodies be established. Such demands were a challenge to Jordan's sovereignty over its citizens of Palestinian origin and to the regime's slogan of "one Jordanian family composed of Transjordanians and Palestinians."

Fortunately for King Hussein, however, he was not obliged to define his position until the proposals received the official sanction of the Arab League. Moreover, knowing that to reject them out of hand would have tainted him with bad faith in the eyes of his Palestinian subjects, he bided his time, maintaining correct, if not cordial, relations with Shuqayri. In May 1964, he even permitted Shuqayri to convene the 1st Palestine National Congress in Jerusalem, at which the Palestine Liberation Organization was inaugurated in the presence of 400 delegates.

The difficulty of eventually having to reject Shuqayri's demands was further compounded, from early 1965 onward, by the more immediate problem of curbing the infiltration of Palestinian fedayeen ("suicide

---

[32]See Kerr, *Arab Cold War,* pp. 127–136.
[33]*Al-Ahram* (Cairo), Sept. 20, 1963; *al-Hayat* (Beirut), Oct. 9, Oct. 10, 1963.

fighters") into Israel via Jordan. In January 1965, Yasir Arafat, who had founded a new and secret organization called al-Fatah (which was independent of the newly formed PLO),[34] finally obtained the aid of a hitherto reluctant Syrian government in carrying out hit-and-run raids into Israel.

The ruling Ba'th party of Syria, after having rejected all of Arafat's previous requests for operational aid, decided in late 1964 that it could exploit its sponsorship of Fatah activity to advantage in its propaganda war against Egypt.[35] Nasser had just scored a point by sponsoring the establishment of the PLO, and one way that Syria could steal the thunder from him was to sponsor more extreme activity, such as Fatah's terrorist operations. With their own national interests uppermost in mind, however, the Syrians forbade Fatah to cross into Israel directly from Syria, thus avoiding the risk of Israeli retaliatory raids. Instead, Fatah activity was directed primarily toward Jordan, from which most of its operations against Israel were staged.

This situation was dangerous for King Hussein, given that Fatah infiltration from Jordan would most certainly lead to Israeli reprisal operations, as indeed it did in May and September 1965. To check this infiltration, however, might have aroused further Palestinian discontent with Hussein's regime; moreover, if discontent became the general mood, it might in turn have weakened Hussein's ability to withstand the demands of Ahmad al-Shuqayri's PLO. In the final analysis, however, the danger of Israeli reprisals seemed greater. Not only did they threaten the territorial integrity of his kingdom, but in the wake of each reprisal raid the Palestinians residing along the border renewed their demands for better arms and for Palestinian officers for the National Guard, which the regime had set up for the defense of border villages under the command of East Bank bedouin officers and NCOs.[36] Hussein, hoping to prevent the occasion for raising such demands (which were so similar to those of the PLO), decided to clamp down on Fatah—but as inconspicuously as possible.

---

[34]The Arabic word *fatah* (strictly, *fath*) means, significantly, "conquest." The three root letters (*f-t-h*), in reverse, are also the abbreviation for Movement for the Liberation of Palestine (*harakat tahrir filastin*).

[35]Ehud Yaari, *Fatah* (in Hebrew). Tel Aviv, 1970, pp. 39–40.

[36]Peter Young, *Bedouin Command with the Arab Legion, 1953–1956.* London, 1956, p. 100; John B. Glubb, *A Soldier with the Arabs.* New York, 1957, pp. 290–291.

The king's dilemma mounted until September 1965 when Arab politics again took an unexpected turn. At the 3rd Arab Summit Conference held in Casablanca, Nasser deserted the PLO. Ahmad al-Shuqayri had asked the conference to empower the PLO to deal only with the Arab League, which would act on behalf of its own member states, with whatever decisions reached through these bilateral negotiations to be binding on the individual Arab rulers. This action would have spared him not only separate negotiations with each ruler but also the concomitant danger that each ruler might obstruct PLO activity in his own country. But the Casablanca Summit Conference under Egypt's leadership rejected Shuqayri's request; thus the PLO would have to negotiate separately with each relevant state. Nasser, realizing that independent Palestinian action necessarily involved factional strife that might implicate Egypt in an untimely war as factions vied with each other in being more extreme, eliminated this escalating competition by withdrawing his protégé, the PLO. He hoped that the Syrians would consequently restrain their own protégé, Fatah.

Nasser's abandonment of Shuqayri signaled to King Hussein that he could now take action against the PLO without the danger of Egyptian condemnation. The king experienced a sense of relief that was already evident in the policy speech he delivered to a joint session of Jordan's parliament on October 4.[37] Striking out at Shuqayri, he asserted that "those organizations which seek to differentiate between Palestinians and Jordanians are traitors who help Zionism in its aim of splitting the Arab camp. . . . We have only one army, one political organization, and one popular recruiting system in this country where the blood of Palestinians and Jordanians were mixed at Bab al-Wad and Kfar Etzion."

Fatah was flayed in the same speech for trying "through improvised operations to push us into war with Israel before we are properly prepared. This sort of activity only helps the enemy. We will not permit it any more. We will not repeat the mistake of 1948. The Casablanca Conference decided on a careful program of preparation for the ultimate day of revenge."

Then, in December 1965 and January 1966, Hussein began to assert his authority, ordering the arrests of both PLO and Fatah personnel.[38]

---

[37]*Filastin* (Jerusalem, Jordan), Oct. 5, 1965.

[38]*Jerusalem Post* (Jerusalem, Israel), Dec. 10, Dec. 30, 1965; *New York Times,* Dec. 30, 1965.

Until June 1966, the surveillance of his army limited Fatah to carrying out only one operation against Israel from Jordanian territory.[39]

By mid 1966, however, the tables were turned once again on Jordan. President Nasser, who had failed to win his ruinous war in Yemen, decided to devote his main efforts to bringing down the regimes of Saudi Arabia (which was backing the Yemeni royalists) and of the Saudis' recent ally, Jordan. In his campaign against the Jordanian monarch, Nasser sought to utilize the Palestinians, as he had ten years previously. For this, he reversed his earlier policy and gave outright political support not only to his erstwhile protégé, the PLO, but to Fatah as well. Whereas in March 1966 Nasser had claimed that fedayeen activity was ineffective and counterproductive, by July of the same year he was advocating that the fedayeen be given the opportunity to shed their blood in the pursuit of their rights. King Hussein, isolated once more and subject to a new and vicious propaganda attack against his throne, felt constrained to soften his repression of Palestinian organizations. One result was that Fatah carried out fourteen operations against Israel from Jordanian territory between June and October 1966.[40]

The futility of King Hussein's position was demonstrated on November 3, 1966, when the Israeli army staged a heavy reprisal raid on the West Bank village of Samu'a, in which 18 people were killed and 134 wounded. Furor was widespread throughout the West Bank; for twelve days crowds rioted in all the major cities, urged on by Egyptian, Syrian, and Iraqi radio broadcasts. The leniency that the king had shown in regard to Fatah and the PLO over the previous six months was obviously insignificant in Palestinian eyes. The rioters, as in the past, demanded better arms, accusing the regime of being unable to defend them. They called for the abdication of the king himself and for the establishment of a PLO government in Jordan.

Order was not restored for two weeks, and the experience cost the king dearly. The need to wield the Arab Legion against the Palestinians wiped away six years of effort to win legitimacy in the eyes of these very people. Although Hussein survived in the end, he was forced to realize that stability and legitimacy were yet a long way off. Meanwhile, the lesson learned from the Samu'a affair was that he had to break out of his isolation in the Arab world and align himself in particular with Egypt and Syria, both of which the Palestinians viewed as their true

---

[39]Yaari, *Fatah*, p. 62.
[40]Ibid., p. 66.

allies. It was the only effective way of neutralizing the Palestinian complaints against his regime. Therefore, when the opportunity to ally himself with Cairo and Damascus appeared on the eve of the Six-Day War, Hussein eagerly grasped it, despite the considerable risks involved in a war with Israel. Whatever the cost, he felt he could no longer allow himself to remain outside the mainstream of Arab nationalism.

TWO

After the Six-Day War

THE LOSS OF THE WEST BANK

Jordan's political dilemma was dramatically highlighted by its disastrous participation in the Six-Day War of June 1967. By May 28, King Hussein had decided that war with Israel was imminent and that Jordan must take part in it. So, despite his conviction that Israel possessed superior power and that Nasser was deliberately provoking hostilities, it was Hussein himself who, on May 30, took the initiative in contacting the Egyptian president and bringing Jordan into a tripartite alliance with Egypt and Syria. Zayd al-Rifaʻi, the king's secretary at the time, described Hussein's motives as follows: "[His] desire to meet with Nasser may seem strange when one considers the insults and abuse which Radio Cairo had been hurling at the Hashimite throne for the past year; nonetheless, *it would have been impossible for us to justify our remaining aloof from so momentous a matter which engaged the entire Arab world.*"[41]

It was a great gamble, but the need to reenter the mainstream of inter-Arab activity was deemed so vital to the internal stability of the regime that even the dangers of war were not too high a price to pay. Other members of the royal establishment were also apparently aware of the need to line Jordan up with Syria and Egypt—for, as Rifaʻi recalled, when the people in the palace learned that Nasser had finally

---

[41]King Hussein, *Our War with Israel* [as told to Vick Vance and Pierre Lauer] (Arabic edition). Acre, n.d., p. 33 (translation of passage and italics by C. B.); cf. English edition of Hussein of Jordan, *My War with Israel.* London, 1969, pp. 40–42.

agreed to accept Hussein as an ally in the forthcoming war, they all "heaved a sigh of relief."

Indeed, the regime's alliance with Cairo and Damascus, and its subsequent participation in the war (which it began by shelling West Jerusalem), ended Jordan's isolation in the Arab world and enabled the king to take his place alongside the other Arab rulers, albeit in defeat. Moreover, in the wake of the fighting, the king was given a prominent role to play in the postwar diplomacy of the Arab world, thus becoming the chief spokesman for the Arab cause among Western nations. At home, in the eyes of the Palestinians and many other Jordanians, Hussein had led the country in a war that all had desired, even though he had led it to defeat. The Palestinians could not continue to single out the king as a special object of blame for the Arab failure. Their hero, Nasser, and their other most ardent advocates, the Syrians, had done no better.

However, all this proved minimal compensation for Jordan's losses and must certainly have raised doubts in Hussein's mind about the wisdom of running such risks just to maintain a proper image at home. In the first place, Jordan's losses in the war itself were heavy. In three days of fighting, the Legion suffered 7,000 casualties—14 percent of its total manpower.[42] More than half of its tanks were lost and its aircraft destroyed, in addition to heavy losses of artillery pieces. It would require great effort to restore the army to its prewar strength and an even greater effort to restore its morale.

More important were the losses of the West Bank and the holy places of Jerusalem and Bethlehem. These had lent great prestige and importance to an otherwise unimpressive state; as before 1948, Jordan might once again be considered an insignificant little desert kingdom numbering barely a million and a half souls. The separation from the West Bank also threatened to cause an economic disaster, for almost 40 percent of the Jordanian GNP had been generated there. In the agricultural sector, the West Bank accounted for 65 percent of the country's fruit and vegetable production and grew 80 percent of Jordan's olives. The loss of the West Bank also meant the contraction of the internal market for East Bank products.[43] While many of these economic consequences were mitigated by the free flow of people and goods under the "Open Bridges" policy established by Israel and Jordan after the war, the overall effect of the loss of the West Bank was of great importance and deeply felt.

---

[42]The following figures and the sources may be found in Daniel Dishon (ed.), *Middle East Record, 1967* [hereafter *MER, 1967*]. Tel Aviv, 1971, pp. 232–233.

[43]Kanovsky, *Economy,* pp. 19–44.

King Hussein's overriding concern in the wake of the war was thus to regain the West Bank. The fighting had hardly ended when he utilized his popularity in the West and embarked on a diplomatic campaign to bring international pressure on Israel to withdraw from the captured Jordanian territory. In return for Israeli withdrawal, Hussein declared himself willing to have the West Bank demilitarized and to offer Israel access to the Jewish holy places in Jerusalem; he was also rumored to have suggested an Israeli enclave at the Wailing Wall similar to the enclave on Mount Scopus.[44] It was similarly reported that in return for withdrawal the king would end Jordan's "state of belligerency" with Israel.[45]

Hussein maintained his intensive diplomatic activity until the end of 1967.[46] During those six months he left Jordan nine times on diplomatic missions, intending to mobilize support for his proposals. Both before and after the Khartoum Arab Summit conference in late August, the king coordinated his campaign closely with President Nasser, who shared his belief that an Israeli withdrawal from the occupied territories could be achieved by political pressure. It was with Nasser's endorsement that Hussein acted as unofficial spokesman for the Arab cause in the West. His mild manner and his record for a relatively moderate approach to the Palestine problem were seen as an effective foil to the fanaticism that had characterized most other Arab rulers up to the war. Therefore, from the point of view of Arab politics, this was a favorable period for King Hussein. Never before had he been so accepted by the Arab world. What better credentials could the Palestinians require than his having been delegated by Nasser himself to represent the Arab cause.

Hussein's mission was doomed to failure, however, because the Arab rulers withheld the one authorization that could have convinced Western leaders that the Arabs had indeed moderated their basic hostility. Hussein was forbidden to offer Arab recognition of Israel or even direct negotiations with it—principles that had been formalized in the Khartoum resolutions of September 1967.[47] The consensus in the West was that the Arabs now had a sufficient stake in moderating their position; to accept their traditional stance of intransigence was therefore unnecessary.

---

[44]*Al-Nahar* (Beirut), Aug. 29, 1967.

[45]*Al-'Amal* (Beirut: Phalange), Aug. 26, 1967.

[46]A good summary of this activity can be found in *MER, 1967,* pp. 255–273, 404–405.

[47]The 4th Arab Summit Conference (at Khartoum), decided (Sept. 1, 1967): "no peace with Israel, no recognition of Israel, no negotiations with it."

Hence, by the end of the year, Hussein realized that his diplomatic efforts were in vain. The West would not help him to regain his lost territory on the terms that the Arab world was imposing; moreover, he was not willing to run the risks involved in assuming an independent position that was contrary to the Arab consensus, especially as Israel's own intentions regarding the West Bank were far from clear.

THE REGIME AND THE RENEWAL OF FEDAYEEN ACTIVITY

The king's concern over the future of the West Bank was shared by Yasir Arafat, though for different reasons. Both men feared that Israel might annex the entire territory as it had done with East Jerusalem on June 28, 1967. As early as July, Fatah began to organize a campaign of terrorism[48] and civil disobedience on the West Bank with two purposes in mind. One was to intimidate the inhabitants there from acquiescing to the Israeli occupation and from making an independent settlement with the Jewish state. The other purpose was to impress upon international public opinion that Palestinians objected to the occupation and would resist all efforts to prolong it or to incorporate the West Bank into Israel.

Arafat himself reportedly crossed the Jordan river in order to organize an underground network of resistance, and in August he launched his operations. By the end of 1967, the fedayeen had carried out sixty-one attacks on Israeli targets.[49] Yet, what Arafat had hoped would develop into a "popular armed revolution" did not take place. Since Israel's security forces quickly found ways of checking terrorist activity, and since the West Bank population was not sufficiently prepared to take risks on behalf of the fedayeen, within five months Fatah was forced to abandon its idea of operating from within the West Bank itself and to seek another strategy for fighting Israel. The price of the West Bank adventure had been high. When Arafat transferred his advance bases to the East Bank of the Jordan River at the end of 1967, about 1,000 fedayeen were in Israeli prisons and another 200 had lost their lives.[50]

---

[48]The term *terrorism* is used in this book to mean acts of violence against civilians or nonmilitary targets, with the aim of impairing national morale.

[49]Yaari, *Fatah*, p. 93.

[50]Ibid., pp. 96, 102.

Nevertheless, the fedayeen activity of 1967 scored a significant political success that overshadowed the military debacle. It was this activity alone that provided evidence of Arab courage in the wake of the humiliating Arab defeat in June and enabled Arabs everywhere to lift up their heads again. Identification with this activism was naturally greater among the Palestinian majority in Jordan than anywhere else, for the fedayeen were Palestinians, the former pariahs of the Arab world, who were now saving its last shred of honor. Not only did fedayeen activity rescue Arab dignity, but it seemed the Palestinians' only hope for keeping their own cause alive, at a time when other problems resulting from the Six-Day War threatened to exclude it from all consideration.

It was against this background that King Hussein was forced to adopt a lenient policy toward the fedayeen movement. To have hampered their efforts or precipitated a confrontation with them would merely have complicated his problems on the East Bank—where the postwar Palestinian component became a majority in the population[51]—and weakened the contact he was hoping to maintain with his Palestinian subjects on the West Bank. Moreover, the king could not deny the advantage that lay in the possibility of widespread and open unrest in the West Bank in protest against the Israeli occupation. If the fedayeen activity succeeded, it would benefit the Hashimite throne by forestalling an Israeli attempt to annex that area.

Consequently, the fedayeen who were in Jordanian prisons when the Six-Day War broke out were subsequently released. Throughout the remaining months of 1967, the fedayeen who passed through the East Bank on their way from Syria to the West Bank did so without obstruction. On the contrary, Hussein even permitted the Palestinian commando unit of the Iraqi army, Regiment 421, to provide active cover for the fedayeen from the eastern slopes of the Jordan valley where it was stationed.[52] What is more, Arab Legion officers who provided cover, intelligence information, and directions to the fedayeen crossing the

---

[51]As the original (i.e., pre-1948) East Bank residents constituted one-third of Jordan's post-1948 population, they would have numbered 700,000 in the total population (2,060,000) in 1966. As the population figure for the East Bank that year—1,140,000—was increased by an estimated 300,000 West Bank refugees from the Six-Day War, Palestinians began to outnumber Transjordanians there in 1967 (figures from Eliezer Shefer, "The Jordanian Economy," *Maariv* [Tel Aviv], Mar. 20, 1970).

[52]Yaari, *Fatah,* p. 166.

Jordan River were not so seriously reprimanded as to feel constrained to stop.[53]

During this period, Hussein's only activity against the fedayeen occurred on the diplomatic level. He attempted to mobilize an all-Arab consensus against fedayeen activity per se; only if and when other Arab countries, and Syria and Egypt in particular, stopped their support for the fedayeen could the regime itself take measures against them. The king's main complaint against the fedayeen was that just as they had involved the Arab states in an untimely war in June, so they would now provoke Israeli retaliations while the weakened Arab states were in no position to defend themselves.[54] Despite Hussein's argument, Syria, who had always advocated a military solution to the Arab-Israel problem, continued to support the fedayeen, and even Egypt saw sufficient value in fedayeen activity to justify endorsing it. The editor of *al-Ahram,* Hasanayn Haykal, later defined the Egyptian position by saying that "the great value in fedayeen action was the fact that both the enemy and the whole world understood that the Arabs continued to subject Israel to fire, albeit symbolic."[55]

The respective interests of the Palestinian organizations and those of the Jordanian regime began to clash openly in October 1967, when the fedayeen attacked Israeli villages in hit-and-run operations from the East Bank. As a result, Israel shelled Jordanian targets in November, causing casualties among the non-Palestinian farming population of the recently developed Ghor valley. Hussein's fears were instantly confirmed: Fedayeen activity would spur Israeli retaliation at a time when Jordan was in no position to defend herself. The clash of interests became even sharper in the early months of 1968 after Fatah, which had been forced to flee from the West Bank, set up its headquarters in Jordan proper and demanded a freedom of action that could be granted only at the expense of Jordanian sovereignty.

THE PALESTINIAN "STATE WITHIN A STATE"

After it became clear to the fedayeen that they could not wage a war of popular resistance against Israel from within the occupied territories,

---

[53]See, for example, *Haaretz* (Tel Aviv), Sept. 6, 1967; M. Naor, *The War after the War* (in Hebrew). Tel Aviv, n.d., pp. 30ff.

[54]*Al-Nahar,* Feb. 20, 1967.

[55]For discussion of this and other Egyptian attitudes, see Harkabi, *Fedayeen,* p. 32; and *MER, 1967,* pp. 214–215.

they moved their forward bases eastward into Transjordan. The new bases were set up in the Jordan valley within close proximity of the river. The main headquarters were situated in the Karameh refugee camp, north of the Dead Sea, which served as a training and supply center as well as a staging position for operations. Smaller bases were set up at other spots in the Jordan valley and along the border with Israel south of the Dead Sea.

The bases in the Jordan valley did not last long, however, for Israeli army operations of March 21, 1968, against Karameh and other fedayeen concentrations proved them too vulnerable to attack by ground forces. Immediately after the Karameh operation, in which the Fatah headquarters were destroyed, 170 fedayeen were killed, and 130 were taken captive,[56] all the bases were moved inland high onto the mountain slopes west and northwest of Amman. From here they could overlook the Jordan valley but were difficult to reach from that direction. The new bases consisted mainly of tents and caves, and emphasis was placed on dispersing the forces. The main headquarters were moved from Karameh to the outskirts of the town of Salt, while other large training, supply, and operational bases were established outside the towns of Amman, Jerash, Irbid, and Ajlun.

Within four months, however, these bases proved vulnerable as well, after Israel began attacking them in surprise air-raids on August 4. Confronted with this new escalation in Israeli operations against them, the fedayeen sought sanctuary in the midst of population centers that they believed Israel would not bomb. Headquarters for most of the organizations were set up on Jebel Husayn inside Amman itself, while supply and training bases were situated in the midst of refugee camps such as al-Wahdat near the Jordanian capital. In order to protect combat units from detection and bombing, they were kept small and mobile and constantly shifted their encampments, in some cases daily.

This transfer of fedayeen bases from the Jordan valley to the hinterland of Jordan exposed the country's population centers to the large-scale presence of fedayeen. Although they numbered only 700 at the outset of their activity on the East Bank, enthusiastic volunteers bolstered their ranks to some 5,000 by the end of 1968 and to 12,000 a year later.[57] Simultaneous with this growth in trained manpower, the organizations

---

[56]For casualty details, see Daniel Dishon (ed.), *Middle East Record, 1968* [hereafter *MER, 1968*]. Tel Aviv, 1973, p. 368.

[57]*Jerusalem Post*, March 22, 1968.

also armed the Palestinians living in refugee camps, intending to form a popular militia. Such an armed force, it was believed, would contribute to the fulfillment of one of Arafat's main tenets—namely, that under the Palestinian popular revolution, the entire population must take part in the struggle. More important, however, was the consideration that a large armed militia of civilians would make it more difficult for the regime to curb the fedayeen.

Arming the population on their own initiative was in itself an infringement of Jordanian sovereignty—but only one among several infringements perpetrated by the fedayeen. The fedayeen also moved about in towns and in the countryside bearing arms and wearing their own camouflage uniforms. Their disregard for the Jordanian authorities was manifest in their refusal to register their vehicles or carry Jordanian license plates; in their enlistment of Jordanian Palestinians eligible for Jordan's national draft; and in their exemption of their members from legal obligations, including the payment of debts and alimony.

These practices were tantamount to extraterritoriality; it was as though the domain of the fedayeen was out of bounds for the Jordanian government. Fedayeen accused of committing crimes were tried by their own courts, and fedayeen patrols and sentries in the cities assumed responsibility for the conduct of their members. Operational bases and staging areas were completely under fedayeen jurisdiction, flying the Palestinian flag overhead. They were fortified and guarded by fedayeen who set up checkposts at points of approach that they deemed sensitive.[58] King Hussein himself was forbidden to enter Fatah headquarters at Salt in August 1968,[59] and on another occasion his brother, Prince Hasan, was barred from entering a fedayeen camp.

The self-assumed autonomous status of the fedayeen organizations was also manifested in the social services that they ran on their own behalf and on behalf of Jordan's Palestinian population. They set up hospitals, dispensaries, and convalescent homes; provided schooling for the children of fedayeen who were imprisoned in Israel or killed; awarded scholarships to Palestinian students studying abroad; and even handled the dispatch of Palestinian teachers to various corners of the Arab world—a matter that had previously fallen within the jurisdiction of the Jordanian Ministry of Education.

---

[58]*Times* (London), Dec. 4, 1968; *Washington Post* (via *Maariv*, Nov. 16, 1969).
[59]*Haaretz*, Aug. 13, 1968.

These manifestations of disregard for the authorities were accompanied by daily occurrences of lawlessness.[60] Fedayeen on leave in town frequently intimidated the local population by firing their weapons into the air. They extorted funds from foreigners in restaurants, hotels, and private homes, and took to cajoling local merchants into making contributions to the fedayeen movement. On several occasions they organized mass demonstrations and disorders that paralyzed life in the capital. They kidnapped Arab political figures, foreign diplomats, and journalists. On other occasions, they precipitated clashes with the police and army by attacking government offices. They also meddled in domestic politics, soliciting the collaboration of oppositionist politicians and even traditional supporters of the regime, including some bedouin.[61]

THE POPULARITY OF THE FEDAYEEN MOVEMENT

These threats to the sovereignty of Jordan were only one aspect of the regime's problems arising from the fedayeen presence. Fedayeen activity against Israel from Jordanian territory posed a danger to the external security of the state itself. Such operations drew reprisals by Israel's army that the Jordanian army was not prepared to counter. By the end of 1969 alone, the fedayeen had carried out 3,170 operations from within Jordan. The majority of these involved mortar-firing on Israeli settlements; a large proportion also involved the laying of mines. By 1970, this activity had taken a toll of some 100 Israelis killed and over 500 wounded.[62]

Israeli retaliation was usually directed at fedayeen positions or those of the Arab Legion that had assisted in a fedayeen operation. On occasion, however, actions inflicting damage on the civilian population were deemed necessary in order to compel the Jordanian government to take more rigid precautions. Such was the artillery shelling of Irbid city in September 1968 in retaliation for the firing of Katyusha rockets into the Israeli town of Beit Shean. More significant were the Israeli strikes against the Ghor valley irrigation canal, which provided water for most of Jordan's agricultural production. In 1968, these strikes caused 70,000 residents

---

[60]*Daily Telegraph* (London), Mar. 28, 1968; see *MER, 1968,* pp. 589–590, for additional details.

[61]One example was a brother of Akif al-Fa'iz, the paramount chief of the very loyal Bani Sakhr tribe.

[62]Yaari, *Fatah,* pp. 237–238.

of the Jordan valley to flee to the highlands around Salt and Irbid, in the process deserting their fields and produce.[63] Although some subsequently returned, further artillery destruction of the canal in 1969 precipitated another flight.

The injury done to the civilian population of Jordan in the wake of fedayeen attacks against Israeli targets naturally created pressure upon the regime to curb this activity; after all, the regime was also responsible for its East Bank citizens. This was precisely the result that Israel desired; the government in Jerusalem was convinced that it was within Jordan's power to curb the fedayeen. The Arab Legion, it argued, numbered 55,000 men who were well-trained and loyal to the regime. The Palestinian organizations, even at their height, numbered no more than 15,000, most of whom were only slightly trained and armed with inferior weapons.

As always, the regime's reluctance to use force was more a question of politics than one of logistics. Second to sovereignty itself, the regime desired to be considered legitimate by the Palestinians; to openly declare opposition to the fedayeen, with the popularity they enjoyed, might alienate the Palestinians irrevocably. Moreover, the attainment of legitimacy was vital now to the monarchy's survival in the East Bank itself. Prior to the Six-Day War, Palestinians had constituted only 40 percent of the population there, subsequent emigrations from the Gaza Strip and the West Bank gave them a 60 percent majority—some 975,000 persons in 1972.[64] To estrange the Palestinians might therefore endanger not only King Hussein's tenuous ties with the West Bank but the very existence of his regime on the East Bank as well.

One manifestation of fedayeen popularity was their ability to attract thousands out of their homes and into the streets for antiregime demonstrations. The funeral procession for fedayeen killed during the Israeli operation at Karameh, for example, was attended by 50,000 supporters. Ten thousand participated in the demonstration that led to the cancellation of a visit to Amman by Joseph Sisco, the U.S. under-secretary of state for the Middle East, in April 1970. Three months later, 30,000 Palestinians attended a fedayeen-organized rally to oppose the Rogers Peace Plan, a

---

[63]*MER, 1968*, pp. 604–605.

[64]Kanovsky, *Economy*, pp. 145–147. This is based on figures compiled by Nabeel Shaath, "Palestinian Professional Manpower," in *Journal of Palestine Studies* 1(2), 1972, p. 81. Shaath reported 900,000 Palestinians living in the East Bank in the late 1960s.

U.S. initiative bearing the name of William Rogers, then secretary of state.

Fedayeen activity against Israel, in general, was sufficient to generate such enthusiasm. But the single event that most enhanced the fedayeen reputation was the battle of Karameh on March 21, 1968. In reality, two battles were fought on that day—at Karameh itself and at fedayeen bases south of the Dead Sea. It was a combined operation that comprised Israeli tanks, mechanized paratroopers, and planes—a fighting force of 1,500. Karameh was captured, in addition to the smaller bases in the south; fedayeen installations were destroyed, some 100 fedayeen were taken captive, and another 170 were killed. Throughout the day, Arab Legion tank units engaged the Israeli force, resulting in casualties to both sides. Twenty-eight Israeli soldiers were killed and 90 wounded. Four tanks and 6 other military vehicles were lost. At the end of the day, the Israeli force withdrew, considering its aims at Karameh accomplished.[65]

The Fatah version of the battle was different. The fedayeen maintained that Israel attacked with a force of 12,000 and suffered 400 casualties, mostly at the hands of the fedayeen themselves. Fatah stressed that although the fedayeen had advance knowledge of the massive invasion, they decided not to flee but rather to stand fast, so as to prove that the Palestinians were fighters and "to prevent yet another retreat in the life of the Arab nation." In inflicting casualties on the Israelis and "forcing the Israeli army to retreat," Fatah spokesmen claimed that they had not only restored Arab honor but had also shown that the Palestinian revolution could accomplish what Arab regular armies had failed to do.

The PLO version of "the defence of Karameh"—ignoring the key role played by armored units of Jordan's Arab Legion—was readily believed by many victory-starved Arabs everywhere and immediately nurtured a fedayeen mystique. The number of volunteers to the fedayeen organizations increased sharply after the battle, and their membership was multiplied seven-fold by the end of 1968.

Although the Hashimite regime felt threatened by the presence, activity, and popularity of the fedayeen, it could not easily find an effective way to limit the dangers they embodied or to rid the country of their presence. The means most often used to counter fedayeen popularity were the least risky—but also the least effective. The regime attempted

---

[65]See *MER, 1968*, pp. 365–373 and 404–405, for details and sources relating to the Karameh operation and its aftermath.

to create the impression that it identified with, and supported, the fedayeen movement. Throughout the buildup of tension that preceded the big crisis of September 1970, the king and his senior officials could be heard to reiterate the slogan "We are all fedayeen."[66] They hoped thereby not only to capitalize on the popularity of the fedayeen movement but also to prevent the regime from being completely overshadowed, even in the eyes of its traditional supporters.

The regime "endorsed" the actions of the fedayeen by asserting "the legitimacy" of their activity against Israel. The Palestinians, it contended, had a legitimate right to fight the Israeli occupation, because they had been displaced by Israeli aggression and had lost their lands, their property, and their resources. It was for this reason that the regime aided them; indeed, their entire enterprise in Jordan existed thanks to the regime's permission. As King Hussein stated in 1968, "The fedayeen movement continues to grow because we want it to grow."[67]

On the other hand, the king maintained the legitimate right also of Jordan and the other Arab states to fight against the Israeli occupation, because Palestine, as part of the Arab homeland, belonged to them as well. Seen in this way, Jordan's aims and those of the fedayeen were identical and deserved equal support from the Arab masses, Palestinians included. Most important, the role of the Palestine liberation movement had to be seen in perspective. Fedayeen activity might play an important interim role by causing the Israeli army to become overextended, discouraging immigration and tourism to Israel, adding to the defense-burden of the Israeli economy, lowering Israeli morale, and encouraging the spirit of resistance in the occupied territories and elsewhere in the Arab world. Yet, the ultimate responsibility for the actual liberation of Palestine lay with the Arab regular armies, including that of Jordan.[68]

THE IMPOSITION OF RESTRICTIONS FOLLOWING ISRAELI RETALIATION

Such efforts to capitalize on Jordan's identification with, and support of, the fedayeen movement were not sufficient to eliminate the danger to the nation's sovereignty and security. At best, they served to obscure

---

[66]See, for example, *Maariv*, Mar. 24, 1968.

[67]*MER, 1968*, pp. 587–589.

[68]Daniel Dishon (ed.), *Middle East Record, 1969–1970* [hereafter *MER, 1969–1970*]. Tel Aviv, 1977, p. 795.

somewhat the conflict of interests that naturally prevailed between the welfare of the state and the welfare of the movement. They were also a useful ploy for maintaining the allegiance of the regime's traditional backers, such as the bedouin, who were only slightly less attracted than other Arabs to fedayeen activism.

Nevertheless, fedayeen activity—against Israel, on the one hand, and among the civilian population of Jordan, on the other—had to be limited. Following Israel's first retaliatory assault on the Ghor irrigation canal in February 1968, for example, the regime became particularly sensitive to developments in the northern Jordan valley. It imposed and reimposed restrictions on fedayeen activity there in March, June, August, and November 1968; April, August, and October 1969; and February and June 1970. In each case the restrictions were imposed in order to achieve a respite from Israeli retaliation and Jerusalem's agreement to let Jordan repair the irrigation canal. On each such occasion, however, the fedayeen unleashed such vicious propaganda assaults against the regime that the restrictions were always either rescinded or ignored—until the need arose to impose them again.

The restrictions demanded that the fedayeen coordinate their crossing into Israel or Israeli-occupied territories with local Arab Legion commanders and that they desist from firing rockets and mortars from the East Bank into Israeli settlements. The fedayeen, however, were intent on resisting these restrictions, which virtually eliminated any opportunity on their part to act effectively or to make strategic plans. The prohibition on shelling across the Jordan was particularly burdensome. Since Israel had developed increasingly effective means to prevent and detect the infiltration of its lines, the shelling of Israeli settlements was often the only operation available to the fedayeen.

The obligation to give advance notice of operations to local Legion commanders was viewed with suspicion. The Palestinians knew that Jordan, like any other Arab state, would try to prevent operations that jeopardized her own interests. They also feared that the Legion might even disclose their impending plans to Israel. Thus, whenever restrictions were imposed, the fedayeen organized such a strong public campaign against yet "another plot to eliminate the resistance" that the regime was forced to back down.

The restrictions imposed along Jordan's southwest border with Israel were more successful. Fedayeen minings and ambushes in the Araba valley brought on the Israeli destruction of fedayeen bases south of the Dead Sea on the day of the Karameh operation, March 21, 1968. It was only in November, however, when Eilat itself was shelled by Katyushas from the Aqaba area, that the Jordanians realized they had to curb fedayeen activity in the south in order to save their only port from possible destruction. In an agreement concluded with the fedayeen on November 16, 1968, all fedayeen activity in the Aqaba area was forbidden, and all other operations in the Araba had to take place no less than ten kilometers west of the Israeli border.[69]

This latter prohibition was soon violated, but a series of actions by the Israelis gradually forced the fedayeen to move their bases back into the mountains of Edom, from which forays into the exposed Araba were too risky to be tried frequently. In the Aqaba area, a momentary laxness in Jordanian alertness enabled the fedayeen, in April 1969, to shell Eilat once again, injuring thirteen people. But an immediate retaliation raid by the Israeli air force on Aqaba impelled the Jordanians to revive the November restrictions. Henceforth they were violated only twice, when ships anchored in the port of Eilat were mined in November 1969 and again in May 1970.

ATTEMPTS TO CONTROL THE FEDAYEEN PRESENCE WITHIN JORDAN

When restrictions on fedayeen activity against Israel were imposed, it was in response to specific dangers to Jordan and its regime. The threat posed by fedayeen conduct inside Jordan was no less acute, but because it was more diffuse it proved more difficult to restrain. Yet, by mid-1968, the fedayeen presence in the cities and the threat it posed to the regime's authority could no longer be ignored. While it was perhaps impossible to exclude them from the cities, the regime found it expedient to try to restrict their presence there.

The first pretext to do so presented itself in October 1968, when Tahir Dablan, the leader of a tiny fedayeen group called the "Battalions of Victory," kidnapped a Syrian opponent of the Ba'th regime who had obtained asylum in Jordan and smuggled him back to Damascus. Responding quickly, the regime issued four regulations on October 10:

1. Fedayeen are forbidden to enter Jordanian cities in uniform and bearing arms.
2. Fedayeen armed vehicles may enter Jordanian cities only with special permission.

---

[69]*Haaretz*, Dec. 4, 1968.

3. Jordanian army patrols may stop, check, and search all fedayeen vehicles and groups.
4. The fedayeen must hand over to the authorities those weapons deemed a threat to Jordan's security.[70]

The announcement of these regulations, however, immediately led to clashes between fedayeen and bedouin troops, which, in turn, resulted in King Hussein's decision to rescind them. As he was out of the country (i.e., in England for medical treatment), he felt the time inauspicious for a showdown.

Upon his return to Jordan, the king was determined to reestablish his authority—and it was Tahir Dablan, again, who afforded him the opportunity, on November 2. During a mass protest demonstration in Amman to mark the anniversary of the Balfour Declaration,[71] Dablan incited an attack on the U.S. Embassy, in which its building as well as other property were seriously damaged. That night, Dablan and members of his tiny group were arrested, and clashes between fedayeen and the Legion ensued, killing some thirty persons, mostly Palestinians. This time, the fedayeen backed down, realizing that the regime meant business.

Subsequent negotiations between the two sides led within the same month to an agreement (hence called the "November Agreements") that contained seven restrictions designed to guarantee Jordanian authority throughout the country:

1. Fedayeen are forbidden to appear in Jordanian cities in uniform and bearing arms.
2. Fedayeen are forbidden to stop or search civilian vehicles.
3. Fedayeen organizations are forbidden to conscript citizens eligible for the Jordanian draft.
4. Fedayeen must carry fedayeen I.D. cards at all times.
5. Fedayeen vehicles must carry Jordanian license plates.
6. Fedayeen crimes will be investigated by Jordanian authorities.

---

[70]*MER, 1968*, p. 592.

[71]Palestinian Arabs hold annual protest demonstrations on November 2 to mark the anniversary of the Balfour Declaration of 1917, which affirmed Great Britain's intention to aid the establishment of a Jewish National Home in Palestine.

7. Disputes between fedayeen organizations and the regime will be handled by a council comprising representatives of the regime and the PLO.[72]

The fedayeen agreed to these restrictions, because the 5,000 men they could then muster in Jordan were as yet no match for the Arab Legion. Perhaps more important, they were unwilling to divert their energies from the growing number of operations they were currently carrying out along the front with Israel. They were successfully getting established and enjoying a high tide of notoriety and publicity as well. In the summer and fall of 1968, the world's major news media began covering their activities and organization in depth.[73] From the regime's point of view, the restraint it exercised by eliminating only Tahir Dablan's group, in November 1968, was in deference not to the strength of the fedayeen but to their popularity. The possible political repercussions of trying to rid Jordan of the entire fedayeen presence were too great for that option to be considered practical.

1969: A YEAR OF MOUNTING TENSION

There were no major armed clashes between the regime and the fedayeen in 1969, but throughout the year tension mounted—tension that was to explode in 1970. The Palestinians—satisfied with other provisions of the November 1968 agreement, which called for operational cooperation between the Arab Legion and themselves—initially honored the restrictions placed on their activities inside Jordan, concentrating their efforts on operations against Israel. Initially, too, the Jordanian government seemed inclined to honor its obligation to aid fedayeen activity—in particular, its operations involving the crossing of the Jordan river.

In truth, however, this aid, which proved to be extensive, was not rendered entirely on the initiative of the regime. Many junior officers in the Legion, posted near the border, began to find it natural and correct to aid fedayeen activity—even without official sanction. In light of their own relative inactivity and the ineffectivenes of the Jordanian government in ending the Israeli occupation of the West Bank, it was difficult for them after a year and a half to ignore the fedayeen example of sacrifice and success. They were aware that, by the end of 1968, some

---

[72]*MER, 1968*, pp. 596–597.
[73]See, for example, *Time*, Dec. 13, 1968, cover story.

1,000 fedayeen had lost their lives and hundreds more were prisoners in Israeli jails.[74]

In the same period, the fedayeen had carried out a thousand or so operations from within Jordan itself, and inside Israel they had become a significant irritant in the daily life of the Jewish population. In late 1968 and early 1969, they managed to terrorize the Israelis by setting off time bombs at the Central Bus Station in Tel Aviv; the shrine of Machpela in Hebron; and the Mahane Yehuda market, a supermarket, and the Hebrew University cafeteria in Jerusalem. Abroad, fedayeen had hijacked an El-Al airliner and attacked others in Athens and Zurich. It was hardly surprising, therefore, that young Jordanian officers along the border were pleased to have a hand in this highly successful anti-Israel enterprise. Consequently, they aided the fedayeen in crossing the river, provided intelligence regarding the deployment of Israeli forces and the location and situation of prospective targets, and provided cover-fire in the event that fedayeen units were detected by Israeli patrols.[75]

Beginning in April 1969, however, the attitude of the regime itself stiffened toward fedayeen operations from Jordan. Early that month a new peace initiative was introduced by the four major powers, the United States, the USSR, Britain, and France—an initiative that many Arabs hoped would bring about an Israeli withdrawal from the occupied territories. Shortly after the initiative was launched, King Hussein went to Washington to inform the new U.S. president, Richard Nixon, that the Arabs would moderate their former positions in order for the initiative to succeed.[76] Hussein, like other Arab leaders, was hopeful that the Republican president would be more willing than was his Democratic predecessor to exert pressure on Israel.

At the same time, the king was exploring other channels through which he might regain his lost territories, including the conclusion of a separate agreement with Israel (despite the injunction against separate agreements laid down by the Khartoum Conference). With this in view, he reportedly met with Israel's deputy prime minister, Yigal Allon, and its foreign minister, Abba Eban, in London during 1968.[77] However, in these contacts, as in his later talks with Nixon in Washington in

---

[74]See *MER, 1968*, p. 352, for the figures.

[75]Naor, *War after the War*, p. 54.

[76]*Time*, Apr. 18, 1969.

[77]Based on conversations with the Israeli officials involved, one Israeli journalist wrote about these and other such meetings in *Maariv*, Mar. 31 and Apr. 6, 1980; see also Eric Silver's article in *The Guardian* (London), Apr. 17, 1980.

April 1969, Hussein suffered from a serious disability. In order to be acceptable as a partner to any peace agreement, he had to prove his ability to put an end to fedayeen activity.

At this juncture, the king's ability in this matter was far from convincing. On the very day that he arrived in Washington for his talks with Nixon, the fedayeen shelled Eilat with Katyusha rockets, wounding over ten persons and inflicting damage to property. The attack, in itself a violation of the November Agreements, was an intentional assault by the PLO[78] on the credibility of King Hussein, lest he succeed in convincing the U.S. president that he could control them. Later that spring and throughout the summer, the fedayeen stepped up their shelling and rocketing of Israeli settlements and industrial plants from their side of the border in a further attempt to discredit the king.

Although Israeli retaliation was heavy, inflicting serious losses on property and life, the Jordanian regime decided to act only after June 22, when an Israeli raiding force blew up the Ghor irrigation canal, vital at that time to most of Jordan's summer crops. A week later, on June 30, the king made widespread changes in top military and security posts. Supreme command of the army was transferred from the king himself to his anti-Palestinian uncle, Lieutenant General Sharif Nasir bin Jamil, so as to allow the Legion to carry out stringent antifedayeen measures without Hussein himself having to assume the responsibility for them.

For a month and a half, Sharif Nasir sought to control fedayeen activity in the Jordan valley. He demanded that the terrorists honor the November 1968 agreement by coordinating their operations with the local army commanders in advance, and by desisting from shelling Israeli targets from across the Jordan. Sharif Nasir also reorganized the army to ensure its loyalty, strengthened the special bedouin combat unit that had been set up to protect the regime, and reportedly even mined the approaches to the Jordan river that the fedayeen commonly used.[79] The fedayeen, on their part, opposed Sharif Nasir's measures in both word and deed. They not only openly denounced the commander in chief, but also engaged in shelling Israeli targets from the East Bank with unprecedented intensity. July and August 1969 were the most troubled months Israel had ever experienced with respect to fedayeen activities.

---

[78]The Fatah and other fedayeen organizations first joined the PLO in 1968; Yasir Arafat became the chairman of its Executive Committee in February 1969.

[79]*MER, 1969–1970*, pp. 803ff.

THE RETREAT OF THE REGIME

In their truculence, the fedayeen organizations were aided by the diplomatic support and media propaganda of Egypt's President Nassér. Having begun a "war of attrition" along the Suez Canal in March 1969, Nasser was keen to have the fedayeen harass Israel from the north and the east. Consequently, he intervened on their behalf, regarding freedom of action in southern Lebanon, in their conflicts with the Lebanese government.[80] In Jordan, moreover, he put pressure on the regime to give the fedayeen a free hand in attacking Israel all along her eastern border.

Once again King Hussein found himself confronted with the old dilemma: Should he secure his internal authority and the territorial integrity of his kingdom at the cost of incurring the hostility of the Arab states and the majority of his population? Or should he defer to the Arab world and the Palestinians, and endure various dangers to his sovereignty and to Jordan's territorial integrity as a result? His decision, as so often before, was to bide his time. So long as his army was still strong enough to deter any overt attempt to take control of the country, he could afford to let events take their course.

The king also felt that by being responsive to Egypt's needs and thereby keeping open his channels of access to Cairo he might earn sufficient credit for curbing the Palestinians in the future, when Israeli retaliation became unbearably heavy. Thus, on August 12, Hussein retreated from his formerly stringent position, and as a gesture of rapprochement with Cairo, he appointed the politician whom Nasser most trusted, Bahjat al-Talhuni, as prime minister.[81] He might have had to swallow his pride, but he wanted to wait for a more favorable opportunity to exert his authority.

Yet, however sound the king's calculations, they had an unsettling effect on the country that could not ultimately be ignored. Even among the original East Bank population, dismay set in. Civilians and soldiers alike began to feel that they were backing the wrong horse. By contrast to the image of a dynamic, popular, and confident fedayeen movement, the regime was a retreating, unpopular, and apologetic institution. As a result, Legion officers again began taking an active role in fedayeen

---

[80]Ibid., pp. 102–103.

[81]On the changing of prime ministers to suit foreign policy shifts, see Bailey, "Cabinet Formation," pp. 108–109.

operations, with the king hardly trying to restrain them until the end of 1969. Moreover, the fire that almost destroyed the venerated al-Aqsa mosque in Jerusalem in late August raised the general level of anger and frustration throughout the country to so considerable a pitch that a policy of restraint on the border with Israel became increasingly difficult to justify.

After overcoming Sharif Nasir's attempts to curb their activity in summer 1969, the fedayeen themselves were feeling increasingly confident. They had succeeded in this first confrontation with the regime since they signed the November Agreements in 1968. They concluded that if King Hussein was allowing them to violate the articles of the November Agreements with their activities on the border, he could not stop them from violating the restrictions on their conduct in the cities either. In the second half of 1969, therefore, great numbers of uniformed and armed fedayeen again appeared in the streets of Amman and other cities, driving unlicensed vehicles, extorting "contributions" from citizens and foreigners, and drafting Jordanians openly into their ranks. Under such circumstances, it was rare to find an outside observer who did not predict the imminent fall of the monarchy.

THE CRISIS OF FEBRUARY 1970

By February 1970, however, there was again ample reason to check the recklessness of the past six months. In December 1969, attacks by the Israeli air force on Jordanian military positions that had been aiding the fedayeen inflicted heavy losses in men and materiel. On January 1, Israeli bombers once again put the Ghor canal out of commission, and Israel subsequently revealed little interest in allowing its repair. Later in January an Israeli ground force attacked fedayeen bases in southern Jordan, remaining in that country for twenty-four hours without a confrontation with the Legion.

The Israeli attacks and the lawless behavior of the fedayeen in the cities impelled King Hussein to impose new restrictions upon the Palestinian organizations. He had also been encouraged during January by the success of the Lebanese Christians, who, in the wake of an Israeli air-raid on Kila village early in the month, forced the fedayeen in Lebanon to undertake to uphold the Cairo Agreement of November 1969. Nasser, feeling at the time that he was losing control over events—in light of heavy Israeli bombing and successful commando raids deep inside Egypt— had given the Lebanese Christians a green light to put their house somewhat in order.

In early February 1970, King Hussein went to Egypt's leader to get a green light for Jordan as well. Upon his successful return to Amman, the king, bearing Nasser's covert approval, issued the following restrictions on February 10:

1. Only authorized officials may remand a citizen in custody.
2. The fedayeen are forbidden to obstruct the work of the public security forces.
3. Fedayeen must carry an I.D. card at all times and show it to the public security forces on demand.
4. Fedayeen are forbidden to shoot fire-arms in populated areas.
5. Fedayeen are forbidden to bear arms in Amman and in other public places and on public transport.
6. Fedayeen are forbidden to store explosives in cities and villages.
7. All fedayeen cars must carry official license plates.
8. It is forbidden to hold gatherings, meetings, and conferences without permission of the Ministry of Interior.
9. It is forbidden to publish newspapers except in accordance with official regulations.
10. Fedayeen are forbidden to engage in political party activities.[82]

Although Yasir Arafat and other fedayeen leaders were away on a visit to Moscow—the main reason for the king's choice of time in imposing the restrictions—the fedayeen quickly organized a campaign to have them abolished. All the fedayeen organizations formed a united executive and military command on the very next day, and by nightfall an all-out confrontation seemed imminent as tank and artillery clashes broke out in Amman, claiming 300 lives. Alarmed by the scope of the casualties, the king decided to back down.

The threat of an all-out clash, which was now anticipated, was too high a price to pay for a showdown. Nasser, too, reportedly warned Hussein against such a clash, thus reneging on his earlier endorsement.[83] Moreover, without Nasser's authorization, the king would not undertake a step that promised to alienate his Palestinian subjects. Trying to obscure the impact of his retreat, Hussein held on the same night a press conference in which he claimed that the restrictions were merely intended to strengthen law and order in the country and were not aimed at

---

[82]*MER, 1969–1970*, p. 796.
[83]*Maariv*, Feb. 15, 1970.

anyone in particular—much less the fedayeen. This—and his concluding ironic declaration, "We are all fedayeen"—caused a round of spontaneous laughter among the journalists, who appraised the situation to be very grave indeed. The announcement a few days later that the king had dismissed his minister of interior (responsible for police and security services), Muhammad Rasul al-Kaylani—whom the fedayeen feared — strengthened the overall impression that the regime had become totally helpless.

THREE

The Expulsion of the PLO

THE ANTI-SISCO RIOTS, APRIL 1970

Although helpless to exert his authority over the popular fedayeen at home, King Hussein was nonetheless active on the diplomatic front; in particular, he was trying to convince President Nixon that the Arabs would, after all, accept UN Security Council Resolution 242 as the basis for an Arab-Israeli settlement.[84] This had been the position stated by King Hussein during his visit to Washington in April 1969, when it was welcomed as affirming the basis of a Four Power Peace Initiative that was then beginning. This initiative itself did not gain much ground, owing to the rivalry between the big powers, but the United States continued to maintain close contact with Jordan in setting the stage for its own forthcoming initiative based on Resolution 242—the Rogers Plan.

In his dealings with the Americans, King Hussein was relentless in stressing one central point: An Israeli withdrawal from the territories occupied in 1967 would spell the end of the fedayeen movement. He told *Time* magazine, while in the United States in April 1969, that "the fedayeen exist because there is injustice to the Arab people. Eliminate the injustice and you will eliminate the need for the commandos."[85] Ignoring the PLO's own ideology, which considered the state of Israel

---

[84]Resolution 242 (Nov. 22, 1967) called for the Israeli withdrawal from territories occupied during the Six-Day War, in return for Arab recognition of, and peace with, Israel.

[85]*Time*, Apr. 18, 1969.

itself to be precisely that injustice to the Arabs, Hussein wished to convince his hosts that an Israeli withdrawal from the West Bank would be so welcome to most Palestinians that they would turn their backs on the fedayeen to attain it; in other words, they would allow him, the king, to curb the fedayeen.

In light of his regime's oft-demonstrated inability to curb the fedayeen, however, the king's claim was not convincing. The fedayeen themselves were known to desire Hussein's lack of credibility in Washington, deeming it an asset they had to guard. The greater the king's credibility, the greater were the chances of a settlement with Israel; such a settlement, in turn, would deprive the fedayeen movement of its essence—its cause. With this in mind, the fedayeen shelled Eilat in April 1969, on the day Hussein arrived in the United States on an official visit. A year later, in April 1970, it was this same reason that led them to instigate disorders in Amman in anticipation of the visit to Jordan of Joseph Sisco, the U.S. under-secretary of state for the Middle East.

Joseph Sisco was on a mission to the Middle East to sound out reaction to the impending U.S. peace initiative. While still in Israel, prior to Sisco's crossing of the Allenby Bridge to Jordan, the PLO organized a mass protest demonstration in Amman that brought over 10,000 Palestinians into the streets of the capital on April 14. The demonstration began quietly but later turned into a riot when fedayeen belonging to the leftist groups—the Popular Front for the Liberation of Palestine (PFLP) and the Popular Democratic Front for the Liberation of Palestine (PDFLP)—directed the crowds toward the U.S. Embassy. There they attacked the embassy building, burned down the United States Information Agency (USIA) offices, and set fire to embassy vehicles. Shocked by the general chaos—which Jordanian security forces did little to suppress—the U.S. ambassador, Harrison Symes, recommended that Sisco cancel his visit to Amman. His recommendation was heeded.

King Hussein was enraged. His hopes of becoming a partner to a peace agreement that would return his rule to the West Bank seemed now to have been dashed. The fedayeen, by instigating riots, had scored a significant victory. Their ability to attack and damage the U.S. Embassy seemed to furnish proof that they could not be controlled. In fact, the riots had been quickly organized and came as a surprise to the authorities. The demonstration had begun quietly despite its size, and had the security forces only been more alert, it was thought, the riots could have been averted. From the king's point of view, in any case, the disorders were not so significant as to justify stopping a major peace initiative before it had begun. However, if Hussein expected the U.S.

ambassador to share his perspective on the situation, he was wrong; Harrison Syme's recommendation canceled the planned visit of Joseph Sisco. To dramatize his indignation, the king resorted to an unexpected measure of unprecedented boldness: He ordered the expulsion of the U.S. envoy from Jordan. Then, to reemphasize the point, he dismissed the two officials whose alleged neglect made the mishap possible—the minister of defense, General Ali al-Hiyari, and the director of general security, General Izzat Hasan Ghandur.

The effects of the episode were less negative than Hussein had feared, however, for President Nixon was sufficiently interested in a unilateral U.S. peace initiative to overlook the Jordanian regime's helplessness at the time. Apparently, the two sides were in accord about making progress toward a settlement, whatever the obstacles. The Jordanians thus began to prepare the ground for such progress, but with great caution. While strengthening the special bedouin combat units that would eventually force the fedayeen into a showdown, the regime spent the rest of April and May 1970 making pro-fedayeen and militant anti-Israel statements in order to foster the impression that the idea of a peace settlement had been dropped.

THE ROGERS PLAN, JUNE 1970

Tension nevertheless built up during May, and in early June it exploded. It began with clashes between fedayeen and Jordanian troops, and after respective funerals were held, each charged with tension, an attempt was made on the life of the king. In retaliation, the Legion shelled fedayeen bases that were situated in refugee camps, inflicting considerable casualties. This, in turn, led to a fedayeen assault on Amman in which shops were looted, the homes of foreigners were raided, and passers-by were beaten. Finally, George Habash's PFLP seized foreign guests staying at local hotels as hostages. The fedayeen barricaded themselves in the city's tallest buildings, where the regime could not dislodge them without a bloody and perhaps widespread clash. On June 10, King Hussein agreed to negotiate an agreement with Yasir Arafat, chairman of the PLO, to which all the fedayeen groups had adhered the prevoius month. Although the agreement provided for the release of the hostages, it proved useless as the PFLP, who were holding the hostages, claimed that Arafat's undertaking did not apply to them. They demanded a larger concession—namely the dismissal of the king's two closest aides, Commander in Chief Sharif Nasir bin Jamil, who had been organizing the special bedouin units in the Legion, and the commander of the 3rd

Armoured Division, Hussein's cousin Sharif Zayd bin Shakir, whose units had shelled the refugee camps. Only after the king succumbed to this demand were the hostages released.

Tension continued to run high in Amman, however, with the two forces poised for battle. To appease the fedayeen even further, Hussein complied with their demand to dismiss a number of officers alleged to have had an active role in the month's shellings. On one point in particular, however, the king would not comply. He refused to disband the special bedouin combat units that constituted his ultimate recourse against the 15,000 fedayeen and the 18,000 Iraqi and Syrian troops stationed in his country.[86] He preferred to live with this tension and to wait it out.

On June 25, when U.S. Secretary of State William Rogers announced his new diplomatic initiative, the Rogers Plan, he brought some measure of relief to King Hussein. The plan called for a cease-fire between Egypt and Israel along the Suez Canal and a renewal of the efforts of the UN special representative, Gunnar Jarring, to attain an overall peace agreement based on UN Resolution 242.

To the Arabs, the proposals in themselves were not novel; they had all been made before. Nevertheless, they believed that the escalation in Russian involvement in Egypt over the previous six months (for example, the installation of SAM-3 missiles and the stationing of Soviet pilots in Egypt) had convinced the United States that it would have to apply more pressure on Israel than ever before to make territorial concessions. Moreover, a new U.S. undertaking to supply a large number of Phantom and Skyhawk planes to the Israeli Air Force was expected to give Washington additional leverage over Jerusalem. In Jordan, therefore, hope ran high that Israel would be forced to withdraw from the West Bank.

Overcoming his personal enthusiasm, King Hussein acted with restraint; he did not hasten to accept the U.S. initiative. Experience had taught him not to act alone on such momentous matters, but rather to obtain the endorsement of Egypt first. Egypt, however, was also not quick to accept the initiative. Though weary of trying to get Israel out of Sinai by force, Nasser had apparently not yet despaired. If he could obtain Soviet guarantees of greater involvement in the fighting with Israel, he would indeed continue his efforts to cripple Israel militarily.

---

[86]That is, 12,000 Iraqi troops and 6,000 Syrian troops (*New York Times,* Feb. 11, 1970) stationed there as part of the Arab League's Eastern Command set up in 1968.

While Nasser explored these possibilities with Moscow, King Hussein exercised caution, making no statements either in agreement or disagreement with the Rogers Plan. In fact, the only step he did take in preparation for his acceptance of the Rogers Plan was seen as yet another political retreat. On June 27, two days after the Rogers Plan was announced, the king appointed a new cabinet under Abd al-Mun'im al-Rifa'i that consisted of eight known supporters of the fedayeen. The key post of minister of the interior was given to Sulayman al-Hadidi, an adherent of the Ba'th party and a close friend of fedayeen leaders Kamal Nasir and Bahjat Abu Gharbiyyah. Other ministers were Antun Atallah and Abd al-Hamid Sayih, both deportees from the West Bank; the bedouin leader Akif al-Fayiz, whose brother had joined the fedayeen and had been killed in a clash with the Legion; and Abd al-Qadir Tash and Salih al-Mu'ashir, both colleagues of the former nationalist prime minister, Sulayman al-Nabulsi.

However, what appeared to be a retreat was in reality an astute political maneuver. Hussein knew that if the Palestinian populace came out in favor of retrieving the West Bank within the context of the Rogers Plan, these pro-fedayeen politicians would not be able to reject it. And if pro-fedayeen politicians accepted the Rogers Plan, what further domestic endorsement would the king need to accept it as well?

THE REGIME TAKES ITS LEAD FROM NASSER

During the first half of July 1970 Hussein, who was waiting for Nasser to decide, bided his time in negotiations with Yasir Arafat over a separation of forces in Amman. On July 14, the two leaders signed an agreement that contained no terms that were not in their first agreement of November 1968. The king undertook to aid fedayeen activities, to allow them freedom of movement, and to discontinue all extraordinary measures against them. The fedayeen, on their part, agreed to acknowledge the ultimate authority of the regime and to obey the laws of the country.

Within ten days, however, Nasser's decision finally came, thereby giving the king the free hand he needed. On July 24, the Egyptian president announced that he was accepting the Rogers Plan. He had spent the first part of the month in the Soviet Union trying to persuade the Russians to step up their military involvement along the Suez Canal. Nasser's efforts, however, were in vain. The Russians apparently convinced him that circumstances obliged him to try the diplomatic alternative to his war of attrition.

Jordan often acknowledged its dependence on Nasser's decision in the following month, and when King Hussein officially accepted the Rogers Plan on July 26, he hastened to send a cable to Nasser declaring: "What you accept, we accept, and what you reject, we reject."[87] In public, Hussein became accustomed to referring to the popular Nasser as "our big brother" and to stressing that in accepting the U.S. initiative, he was merely following Nasser's example.

Once his actions had been endorsed by Egypt, Hussein quickly began to strengthen his position. He appointed to positions of power in the security services and the army the three men whom the fedayeen had forced him to dismiss over the previous six months: Muhammad Rasul al-Kaylani, Sharif Nasir bin Jamil, and Sharif Zayd bin Shakir. The king made other new appointments in the army to ensure that key positions would be manned by reliable officers in the event of a confrontation, and in mid-August he raised the salaries of all regular army personnel. He also arranged to move the Saudi troops, which were stationed in the Araba, to a point near the capital, and he reinforced his own troops in Amman as well.

THE FEDAYEEN REJECT THE ROGERS PLAN

While the regime was thus preparing itself to take advantage of the new situation, the fedayeen were not idle. Their main effort to sabotage the U.S. initiative was to shell Israeli border settlements near the Dead Sea and in the Jordan valley. They hoped thereby to provoke retaliations by Israel's army and to undermine the climate of accord. They also sought to provide Israel with an excuse for rejecting the Rogers Plan—their view of Israeli thinking being that if Jordan was unable, at this point, to prevent fedayeen operations, how could it be responsible for maintaining a cease-fire?

Because the Rogers Plan aroused hopes in the West Bank that an end to Israel's occupation was at hand, the fedayeen were also quick to warn the Palestinian leaders there not to endorse it.[88] They even set up "revolutionary" courts to try all "quislings" in absentia, with authority to condemn them to death.[89] The PLO's propaganda media even allowed

---

[87]*Maariv,* Jul. 27, 1970.

[88]Ibid., Aug. 5, Aug. 8, and Aug. 10, 1970. For West Bank expectations, see editorials in *al-Quds,* Jul. 22 and Jul. 24, 1970.

[89]*Maariv,* Jun. 28, 1970.

themselves to attack Egypt's acceptance of the U.S. initiative, as a result of which Nasser closed the Fatah and PLO broadcasting stations in Cairo on July 27. Egypt's president wished it to be clear that he would tolerate no oppositon to his new policy.

Although all fedayeen were opposed to the Rogers Plan, there were differences among the various members of the PLO on how to block it. Yasir Arafat, the organization's chairman, believed that while the fedayeen should not accept the Rogers Plan, they should also not try to sabotage it. Following his own initial attacks on Egypt's acceptance of the plan and Nasser's prohibition on fedayeen broadcasts from Cairo, Arafat himself began to exercise restraint. When he spoke at a mass rally of 30,000 Palestinians in Amman on July 31, he was careful, while attacking the Rogers Plan, not to name either Egypt or Jordan.

Above all, Arafat feared that the fedayeen movement would find itself rejected by its most important Arab backers if Egypt became more antagonistic toward the PLO. He also argued that the terrorists had nothing to lose by exercising restraint with respect to the initiative, for Israel would not give up its occupied territories in any case. Therefore, if Egypt—and the Arab cause in general—could derive political benefit by accepting the U.S. initiative, the fedayeen were obliged to grant Egypt this opportunity.[90]

More extreme leaders—such as George Habash (PFLP), Nayif Hawatmah (PDFLP), and Ahmad Jibril (the leader of the splinter group PFLP–General Command)—disagreed with Arafat. First of all, they argued, Egypt and Jordan might well reach a settlement with Israel, which would occur at the expense of the "Palestinian revolution." The most the Palestinians could expect from such a settlement—if anything— was a "mini-state" in the West Bank and the Gaza Strip, and they rejected this out of hand. For these extremists, the Palestinians were fighting for a principle—to put an end to Zionism altogether and thus achieve justice for all Palestinians—and not just to set up a Palestinian mini-state. To make any gesture that hinted of compromise with Zionism at this stage would discredit their entire effort. Moreover, too much progress had been made in connection with that effort to risk losing it for a dubious tactical advantage on the diplomatic front.

These differences of opinion about the Rogers Plan paralleled other differences about the very existence of the Hashimite regime. Arafat, the

---

[90]See Arafat's statement to the emergency session of the Palestine National Congress of August 27, in *Le Monde* (Paris), Aug. 28, 1970.

leader of Fatah, believed that the PLO should stay out of Jordanian politics and concentrate its efforts on the war against Israel; he also believed that the fedayeen were unable to undertake the responsibilities of ruling Jordan and to fight a war of desperation at the same time. It was sufficient to enjoy freedom of movement and maneuverability within Jordan—and to achieve this, pressure could be put upon the monarchy. Arafat also felt, however, that if the regime were pushed too far, the Legion would intervene, and that this would be to the detriment of the fedayeen movement.[91]

The more leftist-oriented fedayeen were less inclined to permit the Hashimite regime to survive. In fact, they were ideologically committed to its overthrow: As a "non-progressive" state, Jordan would always betray the Palestinian cause. In general, there could be no return to the Palestinian homeland as long as the Arab world remained under the rule of bourgeois regimes.[92] On a practical level, however, the leftists had always stopped short of declaring open rebellion, limiting themselves to humiliating the regime in actions like the anti-Sisco riots of April and the holding of foreign hostages in June that year.

Nevertheless, throughout July and August, Habash and Hawatmah began advocating a change in the regime. At different times they called either for the establishment of a combat state run by popular militias, the establishment of a Palestinian government to operate alongside the Jordanian regime, or the disbanding of parliament and its reconstitution with pro-fedayeen representatives. Such claims were raised at the Emergency Session of the Palestine National Congress, which was held in al-Wahdat refugee camp near Amman on August 27–28.[93] Whether or not these proposals frightened the regime, they at least provided it with a pretext for acting in self-defense.

BLACK SEPTEMBER, 1970

The regime was similarly aided by acts of lawlessness carried out by the fedayeen—especially the PFLP and the PDFLP—who attacked the central post office in Amman, ambushed army vehicles, and, on September 1, tried to assassinate King Hussein while he was on his way to the airport. As tension grew, both sides took up positions in Amman, and skirmishes

---

[91]Harkabi, *Fedayeen*, pp. 19ff; also *Maariv*, Jul. 31, 1970.
[92]*Le Monde*, Aug. 12, 1970.
[93]Ibid., Aug. 28, 1970.

broke out between the Legion and the fedayeen in the towns of Irbid, Zarqa, and Ma'an. The leftist-oriented terrorists began talking of "the final battle."

Aware of the fact that Egypt and many Palestinians themselves were now behind the king, and that the Legion itself was eager for a confrontation, Yasir Arafat tried to persuade the extremists to moderate their activity—but to no avail.[94] On September 6, the PFLP carried out three airline hijackings, taking a Swissair and a TWA plane to Zarqa and a Pan-Am plane to Cairo. On September 9, they also brought a British BOAC airliner to Zarqa. The fedayeen in general found these operations so spectacular that Arafat felt he could not discredit them and retain his position of leadership. As a result, he joined the extremists.

Paradoxically, the hijackings were to prove the very undoing of the fedayeen. The widely publicized suffering of the passengers on the hot, desert runways and the actual destruction of the planes on September 12 put the fedayeen in so negative a light throughout the world that King Hussein could finally allow himself to strike at them without fear of recrimination. A further pretext, if needed, was the fedayeen take-over of the northern Jordanian city of Irbid, where they set up a "people's government" on September 15. That night, the king decreed military rule throughout the country and replaced his cabinet of civilian politicians with a military cabinet composed of loyal, predominantly East Bank officers. The purpose of the military cabinet was to take responsibility for whatever calamities resulted from this long-awaited confrontation with the Palestinian fedayeen movement. To disguise this intent, a Palestinian officer, General Muhammud Da'ud, was named prime minister.

The civil war—as it came to be called—began in earnest on September 16 as the Legion, which had taken up positions in and around Amman, trained its artillery on fedayeen headquarters and other targets in the al-Wahdat and Husayni refugee camps adjacent to the capital. On the next day, ruthless mop-up operations began in Amman itself to dislodge Palestinian fighters from bunkers and rooftops. These operations, which lasted for ten days, were heavy-handed, causing great loss of life and damage to property. The two refugee camps were almost razed to the ground and buildings were destroyed on top of their occupants. In Amman, most buildings harboring fedayeen nests were summarily shelled. The death toll of Palestinians was estimated to be as high as 3,400.[95]

---

[94]See T. DeJardin, in *Le Figaro* (Paris, via *Maariv,* Aug. 10, 1970).
[95]PLO figures (*MER, 1969–1970,* p. 870).

There had been warnings that the 12,000 Iraqi troops stationed near Mafraq (under the Eastern Command, which had been set up with Jordan and Syria in 1967) would be put at the disposal of the PLO in the event of an all-out clash; however, by the time the civil war began, it was clear that these forces had made no preparations for intervention. On the contrary, they were recalled to Iraq on September 17. The Iraqis were wary of being defeated by the larger Arab Legion. They also feared that their involvement in fighting Jordan might tempt the Kurds to rebel in northern Iraq or the Israeli army to enter Jordan from the west.[96]

Syria, on the other hand, did intervene. On September 20, it sent an armored force of 200 tanks into northern Jordan to reinforce the PLO. The Syrian force was disguised as part of the PLO in order to avert international complications for Damascus. As a result, however, the armored columns could not benefit from Syrian air-cover and were completely exposed when the Jordanian air force attacked them on September 21 and 22. Some 75 tanks were thus destroyed, and on September 23 the Syrian force withdrew to Syria. The fact that Israel, at the United States' request, had reinforced its army on the Syrian border apparently played a role in the Syrian retreat.[97]

King Hussein initially felt unhampered in his operations against the fedayeen because of the support he enjoyed from Nasser. As the scope of their defeat became known in the Arab world, however, diplomatic pressure began to be exerted on Hussein, particularly by Nasser. The Egyptian president had, after all, agreed to let the king "clip the wings" of the PLO sufficiently to eliminate their opposition to the Rogers Plan. But he did not want the fedayeen broken and expelled from Jordan; they were too valuable as a potential source of military pressure on Israel in the event that negotiations under the Rogers Plan broke down. Nasser was also concerned that continued fighting in Jordan might provide a pretext for Israel to renounce its acceptance of the Rogers Plan. Consequently, from September 17 until September 24, Cairo repeatedly called upon King Hussein to call back his troops—but to no avail.

The king, no longer the callow youth intimidated by Nasser that he had been in the 1950s, was quick to appraise the situation. He knew that Nasser could break relations with him only at the risk of having

---

[96]*Le Monde*, Aug. 12 and Aug. 28, 1970.
[97]Marvin Kalb and Bernard Kalb, *Kissinger*. London, 1974, pp. 200–209.

the Rogers Plan nullified. Hussein could therefore take his time. The Syrian attack of September 20 also gave him an excuse for not stopping the war earlier. On September 24, however, the Arab League sent a four-man delegation, comprising the prime ministers of Tunisia and the Sudan, the Egyptian chief of staff, and the Kuwaiti defense minister, which was more successful than Nasser had been in persuading both sides to come to terms. As a result, the king and Arafat agreed on a partial cease-fire, which each announced to his troops on September 25 in separate broadcasts over the radio.

Two days later, both King Hussein and Yasir Arafat went to Cairo and, under the sponsorship of Nasser, signed a cease-fire at the Cairo Hilton Hotel. The agreement contained fourteen points, of which the most important follow:

- Both sides will uphold a cease-fire.
- All extraordinary measures taken before the crisis will be abolished.
- Jordan will support the Palestine liberation movement.
- Both sides will withdraw from the cities.
- The Jordanian civilian police will be the only authority maintaining security.
- All prisoners will be released.[98]

The other provisions of the agreement dealt with the formation and authority of a committee, headed by the prime minister of Tunisia, Bahi al-Ladgham, to implement the terms of the agreement.

On the following day, September 28, Gamal Abdul Nasser died of a heart attack. Many said it was caused by the strain involved in ending the civil war in Jordan.

THE FEDAYEEN ARE FINALLY EXPELLED, JULY 1971

Nasser's death, and the absence of his authority and popularity, was a relief to King Hussein in his continuing efforts to reduce the fedayeen to submission. Yasir Arafat saw in Nasser's death the loss of the fedayeen movement's most influential protector. Syria's recent performance in the civil war had been a humiliation that stripped the country of credit. All the more shameful was the performance of Iraq, whose troops were withdrawn from Jordan without their firing a single shot on the Pal-

[98]Text appears in *MER, 1969–1970*, p. 869.

estinians' behalf. The leader of Fatah felt that the best course for the present was to come to terms with the regime in order to consolidate what remained of the fedayeen position and to renew their activity against Israel.

With this in mind, Yasir Arafat, on October 13, 1970, signed the humiliating Amman Agreement, which confirmed the king's control over his country and imposed upon the fedayeen restrictions that they previously would have rejected:

1. The fedayeen have to disband all their bases in towns and villages.
2. The fedayeen are forbidden to bear arms or appear in uniform in towns and villages.
3. In Amman, the fedayeen may provide their own guards for their leaders and officers only.
4. The fedayeen must obey all the civil laws of Jordan.
5. The fedayeen must conform to Jordan's traffic regulations.[99]

Nothing was required of the king other than to show magnanimity, which he did by granting an amnesty to all fedayeen prisoners and by permitting George Habash and Nayif Hawatmah to return to Jordan—on the condition that they operate within the context of the Central Committee of the PLO.

Despite Arafat's caution, however, the inability of the PFLP and the PDFLP to compromise, even just tactically, was to result in the total elimination of the fedayeen from Jordan within the year. The PFLP and the PDFLP adamantly maintained the position that the Palestinian liberation movement should thwart every further attempt to limit fedayeen freedom of action. This led them to resist every effort to implement the Amman Agreement, which, in turn, gave the regime license to do exactly that.

The stage was thus set for repeated clashes between the determined ultraleftist fedayeen and the victory-flushed bedouin soldiers of the Arab Legion, who exploited every such clash in order to tighten the cord around the PLO's neck. Already in November 1970, such clashes took a toll of over forty-five Palestinians and resulted in the Legion's ousting of the fedayeen from the town of Jerash. In January 1971, further clashes led to an agreement that obliged the fedayeen to surrender to the Legion

---

[99]Text appears in ibid., pp. 874–875.

all the arms that they had previously distributed to the Palestinian popular militias.

Realizing that the regime was determined to rid Jordan of the fedayeen, Arafat tried to prevent this action through a two-tiered policy of not irritating the regime, on the one hand, and soliciting Egypt's support, on the other. Fatah spokesmen, for example, began giving tacit endorsement to Egypt's acceptance of the Rogers Plan.[100] Egypt, for its part, was pleased to reappear as a friend of the PLO in order to reverse its virtual abandonment of the fedayeen during the civil war. Therefore, in February 1971, President Anwar al-Sadat, Nasser's successor, agreed to deliver the opening address at the 8th Palestine National Congress convening in Cairo; later, in March, he permitted Fatah to renew its broadcasting from the Egyptian capital.

But all the support that Arafat had gained from Egypt was no help once the Jordanian regime learned of the resolutions passed at the 8th Palestine National Congress. Again, upon the instigation of Habash and Hawatmah, the Congress passed a resolution officially designating Transjordan as part of Palestine. In other words, the fedayeen were saying that the East Bank, no less than Palestine proper, had to be liberated from its present regime and placed under "popular Palestinian rule."[101] This was tantamount to an official declaration of war against the Hashimite regime in Jordan, which was quick to pick up the challenge.

From then on, events moved quickly. At the end of March, the Legion drove the fedayeen from Irbid, where they had set up their "people's socialist republic" in September 1970. In early April, stern warnings by King Hussein sufficed to impel the PLO to remove all the fedayeen from Amman and to relocate them in the wooded hill country between Jerash and Ajlun. There they entrenched themselves in preparation for further confrontations, which they precipitated themselves—by ambushing patrols, sabotaging installations, and attacking civilians, actions that took the lives of twenty civilians and sixteen soldiers and wounded some seventy others.[102]

On July 13, the Legion began its final assault on the 2,500 fedayeen that still remained in the Ajlun hills and the Jordan valley. Within five days—by July 18—the army had routed them out of their trenches and

[100]Y. Harkabi, *Palestinians and Israel.* Jerusalem, 1974, pp. 145ff.

[101]Ibid., pp. 131–144; *al-Anwar* (Beirut), Mar. 5, 1971.

[102]*Keesings Contemporary Archives* (London) [hereafter *Keesings*], 24770 (Aug. 14–21, 1971).

bunkers with artillery barrages and intense machine gun fire. Many were killed and over 2,000 arrested. Those who could—some 200—crossed the Jordan river to surrender to the Israelis rather than run the risk of being caught by Hussein's angry bedouin. By July 19, 1971, the Palestine Liberation Organization ceased to exist in Jordan. By way of explanation, Prime Minister Wasfi al-Tall said, "They violated our hospitality."[103]

KING HUSSEIN'S FEDERATION PLAN

From July 1971 until October 1973—when the "Yom Kippur War" broke out—Jordan enjoyed a period of peace and stability it had never known before. Only two major plots against the regime occurred during that period. The first, in November 1971, came about when Wasfi al-Tall—who had been the driving force behind the liquidation of the PLO in Jordan—was assassinated in Cairo by the "Black September" section of Fatah. Foiled in advance was a second plot, sponsored by Libyan President Mu'ammar al-Qaddafi in November 1972, in which an armored brigade commander, Colonel Rifa'i Hindawi, was supposed to carry out a coup d'état.

King Hussein's Palestinian subjects, understanding that Hussein's decisive victory over the fedayeen had made him master of the situation, fell into line. So complete was their reconciliation with the regime, in fact, that a *New York Times* reporter was led to observe that "Arabs do not admire losers."[104] In the West Bank, where in September 1970 King Hussein was loudly and generally denounced as a butcher and a traitor, his supporters won an overwhelming victory over his opponents in the municipal elections held there in the spring of 1972.[105]

On the East Bank, too, people began putting their lives back into order after four years of tension and strife. The East Bank economy recovered quickly, as reflected in the 43 percent increase in exports and the 25 percent increase in imports during 1972. Jordanians continued to enjoy foreign products at low prices, financed by foreign aid. Although Libya and Kuwait stopped submitting their annual payments to Jordan ($50,000,000 [£20.8 million], as agreed upon at the Khartoum Con-

---

[103]*New York Times,* Jul. 20, 1971.

[104]Eric Pace, "No Longer Standing Proud and Tall," *New York Times,* Jul. 18, 1971.

[105]The major exceptions were the mayors of Ramallah, al-Bireh, and Tulkarm. See Sha'ul Mish'al, "Anatomy of Municipal Elections in Judea and Samaria," *Ha-Mizrah He-Hadash* 24(1–2) (in Hebrew), 1974, pp. 63–67.

ference in October 1967), the United States made good the sum. The income from trade that was lost when Syria and Iraq closed their borders with Jordan in July 1971 was made up by loans from the International Monetary Fund (IMF).

The "ordeal by fire" that King Hussein had undergone left him feeling confident—so confident, indeed, that he dared put forward his Federation Plan on March 15, 1972. Addressing an assembly of 400 Jordanian public figures, the king expounded his vision of Jordan after a peace settlement was reached with Israel. He proposed changing the name "Jordan" to the United Arab Kingdom. This kingdom would comprise two autonomous provinces: the East Bank and the West Bank. Each province would have a separate locally chosen governor, government, and parliament to deal with all matters other than foreign affairs, defense, and the unity of the kingdom. These domains would be handled by a central government and parliament, based on the equal representation of each province. The kingdom would have one united army, and its capital would be Amman.[106]

Reaction to King Hussein's Federation Plan throughout the Arab world was bitter. Hussein was accused everywhere of betraying the Palestinian cause. By proposing autonomy as a solution to the Palestinian problem, he was calling for an end to Palestinian hopes for self-determination and independence; he was proposing to kill the real Palestinian issue. Not only was this harmful to the Palestinian cause, but it deprived the overall Arab cause of its most effective political card.[107]

Cairo severed diplomatic relations with Amman in protest against the plan. Insofar as Jordan's relations with Algeria, Libya, Syria, and Iraq were already broken (since Black September), it found itself isolated from all the important Arab countries except Saudi Arabia. Two years previously such a situation would have been unbearable. Now, however, the king could afford to ignore it, primarily because the Palestinians within Jordan had become quiescent. The major Arab states had proven to them as well as to the king of Jordan that they were neither willing nor able to take effective action on the Palestinians' behalf. Hussein also

---

[106]Text appears in *Keesings*, 25191 (Apr. 8–15, 1972).

[107]The occupied territories were perhaps the only Arab area in which the Federation Plan was not rejected out of hand. On March 20, 1972, the East Jerusalem daily, *al-Quds*, urged the Palestinians to study the plan objectively. See Clinton Bailey, "Changing Attitudes toward Jordan in the West Bank," *Middle East Journal* 32(2), 1978, p. 161.

knew that he wielded a powerful army that had proved itself both loyal and effective. In the long run, moreover, he was certain that the Arab Legion was potentially more of an asset to the Arab cause than was the PLO—a fact that the Arab states would eventually have to acknowledge.

They did exactly that, in fact, just before the Yom Kippur War of October 1973. Contrary to what had happened on the eve of the Six-Day War, when King Hussein rushed to Cairo on his own initiative to offer his services to the ruler of Egypt, it was now President Sadat and Syria's Hafiz al-Assad who took the initiative by inviting Hussein to Cairo for reconciliation talks on September 10. Although they refrained from confiding to the king information about their war preparations, they wanted to be sure of the Jordanian monarch's friendship.[108] On September 23, Cairo renewed its diplomatic relations with Amman, and on October 4, the day preceding the war, Syria hastened to do so, too. Jordan, except for one armored brigade sent to Syria, did not participate in the Yom Kippur War. But it was in a position to benefit from the political atmosphere that prevailed after the war.

---

[108]Kalb and Kalb, *Kissinger,* p. 453.

FOUR

In the Wake of the 1973 War

THE PLO EMERGES FROM THE WAR IN AN ADVANTAGEOUS POSITION

The six years preceding the Yom Kippur War were marked by efforts on the part of the Jordanian regime to counter the challenge of the Palestine Liberation Organization inside Jordan; the ten years following that war were characterized by its efforts to counter the challenge of the PLO in the international arena. These latter years differed from the previous twenty-five years of the Arab-Israel conflict in that the war led to diplomatic activity that broke the impasse of lack of contact and compromise between the Arab states and Israel. Officially, this activity stemmed from UN Security Council Resolution 338, which established the cease-fire on October 22, 1973. According to Section 3 of the resolution, the Security Council decided that "immediately and concurrently with the cease-fire, negotiations will start between the parties concerned . . . aimed at establishing a just and durable peace in the Middle East."[109] More significantly, however, the diplomatic activity of the following ten years stemmed from the military stalemate in which the war had ended. Both sides, appalled by the high human and financial costs of the war and yet proud of their respective achievements in it, emerged more amenable to negotiation than ever before. Despite Jordan's merely token participation in the war, the country seemed at first to be in a position to benefit from it politically. The main clause of UN Resolution 338 called, after all, for the implementation of UN Resolution

---

[109]*New York Times*, Oct. 23, 1973.

242 of 1967, which guaranteed the restoration of Jordan's former sovereignty and territorial integrity in the West Bank.

In fact, it became apparent shortly after the war that Jordan's status as potential sovereign in the West Bank was not at all certain. At the 6th Arab Summit Conference held in Algiers in November 1973, the Arab heads of state passed a secret resolution recommending that the PLO be recognized as the sole and legitimate representative of the Palestinian people.[110] The implementation of this resolution would mean that in Arab eyes, the PLO, rather than Jordan, was responsible for recovering the West Bank. The resolution reflected two parallel sentiments prevalent in the Arab world. First, the Arab states appreciated the fact that the PLO's popularization of the Palestinian cause had brought considerable benefit since the Six-Day War to the overall Arab cause. Second, they held the Hashimite regime in contempt for so often flouting Arab consensus. The list of grievances was long: Black September in 1970, the expulsion of the PLO in 1971, King Hussein's Federation Plan in 1972, and, finally, Jordan's abstention from true participation in the Yom Kippur War.

Paradoxically, it was Israel that rescued Jordan's status from the ill-will of the Arab states in the early stages of negotiations, when preparations for the ceremonial inauguration of the Geneva Peace Conference in December 1973 were being made.[111] President Sadat, who considered the Arabs' position strong enough to introduce the PLO into the postwar diplomatic activity, initially conditioned Egypt's own participation in the conference on that of the PLO. Israel, however, rejected the Egyptian condition, insisting that only by consent of the four participants in the previous war of 1967—Israel, Egypt, Syria, and Jordan—could any additional party be invited. Faced with Israel's adamant stand, Egypt backed down, whereupon U.S. Secretary of State Henry Kissinger went to Amman to invite Jordan to take its place at the ceremonial opening. King Hussein accepted Kissinger's invitation with great relief.

Once at the Geneva Peace Conference, Jordan took full advantage of the opportunity to establish its credibility as a dedicated defender of the Palestinian cause. The address delivered by Premier Zayd al-Rifa'i, now Jordan's foreign minister, was notably more vitriolic against Israel

---

[110]Eric Rouleau, "The Palestinian Quest," *Foreign Affairs* 55(2), 1975, pp. 278–279.

[111]Matti Golan, *The Secret Conversations of Henry Kissinger.* New York, 1976, pp. 125–127.

than that of his colleague, Ismail Fahmi of Egypt. He not only demanded Israel's full withdrawal from all occupied territories, including Jerusalem, and the restoration of all Palestinian national rights, but he also raised the question of Israel's right to exist. He termed the Jewish state a "foreign body in the Eastern Mediterranean," and accused Israel of killing and torturing Palestinians in the West Bank.[112]

Rifaʻi's performance, however, did not have the desired effect on Egypt, because that country soon found itself in need of Jordan's rival, Yasir Arafat. On January 18, 1974, when Egypt signed a disengagement-of-forces agreement with Israel, Egypt came under harsh criticism from both Syria and Jordan. The fact that Sadat would negotiate with Israel without coordinating his position with the other Arab states signaled that in the future Egypt might continue to pursue its own diplomacy, abandoning its weaker sister-states to their own individual resources. To blunt the edge of the criticism hurled at him from the Arab states, Sadat courted the endorsement of Fatah and its leader Yasir Arafat, who responded by refraining from condemnation of the Egyptian-Israeli agreement.[113] In return, Egypt undertook to promote the PLO's international standing. One result of this support was a resolution passed in February 1974 at the Islamic Heads of State Conference held in Karachi, Pakistan; like the resolution taken in Algeria the previous November, it recommended the recognition of the PLO as the sole legitimate representative of the Palestinian people.[114]

To curb this tide of events, which were to Jordan's disadvantage, King Hussein spent March and April visiting Arab and non-Arab capitals in an effort to dissuade his various hosts from supporting, at Jordan's expense, the claims of the PLO. His travels took him to London, Washington, Cairo, Damascus, and Riyadh. In the Arab capitals his most important argument was that the Arabs' best chances for recovering the West Bank lay with Jordan. The king stressed that, while significant elements in the Israeli population—including the country's leading dailies, *Haaretz* and the *Jerusalem Post*—advocated a settlement with Jordan based on an Israeli withdrawal, few Israelis could be induced to support the idea of surrendering the West Bank to the PLO.

Although the Arab rulers with whom Hussein spoke remained unimpressed, the king was not disheartened. With faith in his own appraisal

---

[112]Ibid., p. 135.

[113]*Haaretz*, Jan. 22, 1974.

[114]D. L. Price, "Jordan and Palestinians: the PLO's Prospects," *Conflict Studies* 66 (1976), p. 1.

of the situation, he felt that his Arab counterparts would ultimately be forced to acknowledge Jordan's importance to the success of Arab diplomacy. In order to drive home his point, he decided to confront them with the possibility that the Jordanian option might disappear altogether. He hoped this emphasis would make them more realistic. On May 1, 1974, he made the following statement in his May Day speech: "We shall respect the unanimous Arab will, if it is the wish of the Arab states and their leaders to create a new situation, giving the P.L.O. sole responsibility for the restoration of the occupied Palestinian territory. If the Arab brothers adopt such a decision, then we shall have no alternative but to respect their unanimity, considering it as relieving us of our responsibilities."[115] This challenge to the Arab world did not bring Hussein the desired results. The reactions to his willingness to forgo "his role" were generally favorable.

THE PROPOSAL FOR A JORDANIAN-ISRAELI DISENGAGEMENT AGREEMENT

The U.S. secretary of state, however, was concerned with this turn of events. Kissinger had already realized that Israel would not deal with the PLO and hence had given Prime Minister Golda Meir a secret guarantee that the United States would veto any invitation to the PLO to participate in the Geneva peace talks without Israel's consent. He knew that the United States' ability to continue its diplomatic initiative in the Middle East by moving the different sides toward a peace agreement depended on its ability to keep the options realistic. To do this, it was vital to keep Jordan in the picture. Accordingly, when Kissinger visited Amman later in May to brief the king on his progress toward effecting a disengagement agreement between Syria and Israel, the two statesmen drew up a new plan of action.

The strategy that they adopted was divulged immediately after the signing of the Syrian-Israeli Disengagement of Forces Agreement on May 31, 1974. In an interview with *Newsweek* magazine on June 6, King Hussein called for a disengagement on the Jordan-Israel front as well. He proposed that the Israeli army withdraw to a distance of about ten kilometers—that is, to the hills overlooking the Jordan valley—while continuing to maintain checkpoints at the Damiyah and Allenby bridges.

---

[115]BBC, *Summary of World Broadcasts*, ME/4590/A/3, May 3, 1974.

A similar withdrawal with checkpoints would be effected east of the river by Jordan.

King Hussein's interview was timed to coincide with the planned visit of President Nixon to the Middle East in mid-June. Nixon's visit, occurring immediately after the conclusion of the agreements between Israel, on the one hand, and Syria and Egypt, on the other, was intended to highlight the success of this U.S. administration in breaking the diplomatic impasse in the Arab-Israel conflict, and in reasserting the United States' influence in the Arab world. These were achievements considered vital to Nixon in his struggle to remain in office in the wake of the Watergate affair. To consolidate them, however, it was imperative to effect new agreements (e.g., for a disengagement along the Jordan river) between the Israelis and the Arabs. When the U.S. president and his secretary of state arrived in Israel from Egypt, they broached the subject with the new premier, Yitzhak Rabin, and his Labor party–led coalition government. Nixon and Kissinger argued that it was in Israel's advantage to deal with King Hussein at the present time, rather than to ignore him and have to deal with Yasir Arafat later. In support of their thesis, they brought with them a message from President Sadat warning that procrastination vis-à-vis Jordan would lead to all-out recognition of the PLO's claims to represent the West Bank and the Gaza Strip.[116]

Yitzhak Rabin, however, was not receptive to the U.S. proposition, and in order to shield himself from his guests' pressures he hastened, while Nixon and Kissinger were still in Israel, to pledge himself publicly to the undertaking of Golda Meir's government not to cede any part of the West Bank without a prior referendum. Rabin could now argue that to broach the subject of disengagement with Jordan would be impolitic, even for the United States. If the weakened Labor party had to return to the polls so soon after the disastrous Yom Kippur War and on so sensitive a subject as the West Bank, less compromising elements in the Israeli political spectrum, such as Menachem Begin's Likud party, would gain strength.

Although Nixon and Kissinger left Israel without a commitment, they reassured King Hussein in Amman that their plan would yet succeed. Upon their return to Washington, the administration unleashed the two weapons that Israel most feared. One was U.S. recognition of the PLO. In July, for example, Under-Secretary of State for Middle Eastern Affairs

---

[116]Golan, *Secret Conversations*, pp. 217–218, for the following account.

Joseph Sisco, testifying before the Foreign Affairs Committee of the House of Representatives, expressed the opinion that Yasir Arafat had disavowed the use of terrorism in favor of diplomacy and that the PLO was likely to agree to participate in the Geneva Conference.

The second weapon was the U.S. administration's ordering of a delay in scheduled arms deliveries to Israel. Although Kissinger explained, in reply to Israeli queries, that U.S. policy regarding the PLO had not changed, and that the delays in arms shipments were due to technical and bureaucratic problems, it was clear that pressure was being applied. The United States wanted a favorable Israeli response to its proposition for a Jordanian-Israeli disengagement agreement before King Hussein's scheduled visit to Washington in August.

Meanwhile, equipped with these signs of U.S. support, King Hussein went to Egypt in July to try once again to enlist Arab support for Jordan's essential role in the Arab diplomatic campaign. This support, if he could obtain it, would in turn aid him in Washington. Meeting with President Sadat in Alexandria on July 18, the king declared that he was about to recover another significant strip of Arab territory from Israel. Therefore, if the Americans themselves considered the move to be in their own national interest, would it not be tragic if it were the Arabs who sabotaged it? Furthermore, he urged, in order to hold the Americans to their plan, it was incumbent upon Jordan to prove that the Arab world considered it the party responsible for the West Bank. If that could not be established, Israel could not be induced to cede any part of the West Bank; nor would the United States feel justified in pressing it to do so. The king's thesis was apparently convincing enough for Sadat to give it a chance. Therefore, in the statement concluding their meeting, the Egyptian president gave his endorsement to "a separation of forces agreement on the Jordanian front." This was strengthened by another passage in the statement defining the PLO as representative of all the Palestinians "living outside of Jordan." In its ambiguity as to whether this included the West Bank or not, the passage left the door open for Jordan's participation in the Geneva Conference. The Hussein-Sadat statement also endorsed a role for the PLO at the conference, but the organization's participation was called for only "at the proper stage."[117] This reversal of Egyptian policy could already be looked upon as a breakthrough for the U.S.-Jordanian strategy.

---

[117]*Al-Quds*, Jul. 19, 1974.

Hussein's success in Egypt, however, signaled a warning in Jerusalem. If Sadat was willing to risk his good relations with the PLO by backing the plan for disengagement along the Jordan river, the Egyptian president was apparently optimistic about its prospects. Rabin and his cabinet feared that a major factor in this optimism might be Israel's own undefined policy. Having left the question open since President Nixon's visit to the Middle East, they understood how observers might have been justified in believing that Israel's reservations were not so strong that they could not be eliminated. Therefore, before Israel's Foreign Minister Yigal Allon departed for a scheduled visit to Washington on July 22, Israel had to define its position clearly. Hence, on July 21 the cabinet took up the subject. The policy that emerged stated that while Israel was willing to negotiate with Jordan, it would only negotiate for a final—and not an interim—settlement. As Jordan had not participated in the Yom Kippur War, it was unnecessary to negotiate a separation-of-forces agreement with that country.[118]

Kissinger immediately realized that the new Israeli position was impracticable. Jordan could not negotiate a final settlement with Israel independently of the other Arab states, for they would brand whatever concessions the Hashimite kingdom might make as treason, creating untold and perhaps fatal political difficulties for it; at the same time Israel would not conclude with Jordan a final settlement that did not provide for some territorial adjustments that it would deem vital to its security. The Israeli cabinet's position thus promised to produce a stalemate in the diplomatic momentum in the Middle East, so that when Yigal Allon came to Washington in late July, the U.S. secretary of state sought a compromise solution. Referring to an idea discussed in the Israeli press—according to which Israel, while not withdrawing its army from the Jordan valley, would permit the Jordanians to establish a civil administration in Jericho (the only Arab population concentration in the area)—Kissinger came up with his own Jericho Plan. He proposed to Allon that instead of turning Jericho over to Jordanian administration, Israel might withdraw ten kilometers from the river and turn the entire evacuated area over to UN trusteeship. It was obvious that what the Americans wanted was an Israeli withdrawal, however limited. They felt that their influence in the Arab world depended upon their ability to attain it. When Allon referred the Kissinger proposal to Jerusalem, however, Prime Minister Rabin would not budge. His reply to Kissinger

---

[118]See Golan, *Secret Conversations*, pp. 220–226, for the following account.

was that any withdrawal in the West Bank would necessitate a referendum, which the Labor party could not afford to hold.

Kissinger was still determined. If necessary, he would wage a war of attrition against Rabin, and he had the means with which to do it. He immediately ordered scheduled shipments of tanks and other arms to be held up, their release to be linked directly to Israel's acceptance of the disengagement plan. He then put the United States' full diplomatic support behind the plan. When King Hussein visited the new U.S. president, Gerald Ford, in August 1974, the statement issued after their meeting indicated that "consultations between the United States and Jordan will continue, in order to take up at an early and convenient date, problems that are of special concern to Jordan, including an Israeli-Jordanian agreement for a disengagement of forces."

However, as Kissinger was later to confess to King Hussein, the United States had miscalculated its "manipulative capabilities."[119] All the pressures that Washington could possibly apply to Jerusalem had proved ineffective, and when Yitzhak Rabin visited the U.S. capital in early September, he remained firm in his government's position. For all intents and purposes, therefore, Jordan's hopes for a disengagement agreement with Israel were dead.

THE ROAD TO RABAT

While Jordan was trying to retain its status as the legal sovereign in the West Bank, the PLO was laboring to usurp that status for itself. Whereas Jordan was having difficulty convincing others to let it go to Geneva, the PLO's difficulty was in convincing itself to go. Yasir Arafat, the chairman of the PLO, was inclined to have the organization participate. Not to do so, in his opinion, would be to forfeit the West Bank to Jordan in the event that a settlement was indeed reached with Israel. A refusal to go to Geneva might also alienate the PLO from Egypt, which wished to utilize the peace conference to consolidate the diplomatic advantages gained by the Arabs in the 1973 war. Not to participate would also detract from the effect of a united Arab front.[120]

---

[119]Edward R. F. Sheehan, "Step by Step in the Middle East," *Foreign Policy* 22 (Spring 1976), p. 47.

[120]See Harkabi, *Palestinians*, pp. 270–282, for the following account of the debate held at the 12th Palestine National Congress and of the resolutions adopted by the Congress.

Those opposed to PLO participation at Geneva—in particular, the leaders of the PFLP (George Habash), the PFLP-GC (Ahmad Jibril), and the Iraqi-backed Arab Liberation Front (Abd al-Wahhab al-Kayyali)— argued that PLO acceptance of UN Security Council Resolution 242 would not necessarily negate the Jordanian claims to sovereignty over the West Bank, but instead would legitimate them. Moreover, why should the PLO facilitate a peace settlement that would accord recognition to Israel? What would become of the PLO's entire ideology based on armed struggle? How could the PLO conclude a settlement with Israel and then continue to fight that country?

Arafat sought to assuage the fears of those who rejected PLO participation at Geneva by assuring them that there would be no settlement. The Arabs would demand conditions that Israel could not accept. They would demand the restoration of Palestinian rights, including the right of the refugees to return to their lands. If Israel were to agree to that, half of its population would be displaced and homeless. Also, to ensure the security of the Palestinian Arab state, the Arabs would demand that Israel's "Law of Return" be abolished and that Jewish immigration to Israel be halted. As immigration was the life-blood of Zionism, Israel would have to reject this demand, too.

In any case, Arafat argued, even if a settlement were reached, Israel's return to the pre-June 1967 borders would weaken its morale and military capability to such an extent that no formal guarantees would be able to redeem the country. After that, the Palestinians would be able to demand a return to the borders defined by the UN Partition Plan of November 1947. Even the Soviet Union recognized the legitimacy of the 1947 borders, and would be likely to support the Palestinians' demands to return to them if the PLO went to Geneva.

Arafat also believed that it was possible to draft a PLO position that would not rule out the organization's participation, but would also not affirm the basis of the Geneva Peace Conference—namely, Resolution 242, which called for a halt to belligerency and the recognition of Israel. This assumption was realized in June 1974, when the 12th Palestine National Congress met in Cairo to discuss the very question of the Geneva Conference. The ten-point program that the Congress adopted established the right of the PLO to set up an independent entity in any part of the "Palestinian land" evacuated by Israel, but it also reserved the right to continue the armed struggle to destroy Israel from within that entity. The important points in this "stages" program follow:

• The PLO rejects Resolution 242 as a basis for Arab or international dealings (article 1).

- The PLO will struggle by all means to establish an independent and *fighting* authority on every part of Palestinian land to be liberated (article 2).
- The PLO opposes the establishment of any Palestinian entity that must recognize Israel or renounce any Palestinian national rights (article 3).
- The PLO will use any liberation step as a stepping-stone to achieve the Palestinian Democratic State (article 4).
- The PLO's independent state will work with the other confrontation states to liberate all of Palestinian soil (article 8).

It was further decided that the PLO leadership was unable to negotiate a settlement at Geneva or elsewhere without prior authorization by the Palestine National Congress.

As explicit as the PLO program was in regard to its hostile intentions toward Israel, it served PLO supporters as "proof" that the organization was prepared to participate in a Geneva Conference and to recognize Israel. It was argued that the willingness of the PLO to set up a government in whatever parts of Palestine that Israel was to evacuate meant in essence that it would come to Geneva, as only in Geneva would negotiations be held that might lead to an Israeli evacuation. Furthermore, it was claimed, participation at Geneva would, ipso facto, require prior acceptance of Resolution 242, which, in turn, provided for the recognition of Israel. PLO supporters stressed that the organization only refrained from publicly accepting the UN Security Council Resolution because it defined the Palestinian situation as a refugee problem rather than as a national one. They added that the PLO would acknowledge Israel's right to exist as a nation only after Israel acknowledged the existence of Palestinian national rights.[121]

In August 1974, two months after the 12th Palestine National Congress, Yasir Arafat went to Moscow as the head of a PLO delegation that was received by the Communist party and the Soviet government as an official guest. Since no previous PLO delegation to the Soviet Union had been accorded that status, this honor signified a new common interest between the PLO and the Soviet Union. The Soviet Union was displeased with the recent U.S. diplomatic success in arranging the Egyptian and Syrian

---

[121]For example, see Rouleau's "The Palestinian Quest," pp. 280–282; see also Muhammad Y. Muslih, "Moderates and Rejectionists in the Palestine Liberation Organization," *Middle East Journal* 30(2), 1976, pp. 128–134.

disengagement agreements with Israel, whereas the PLO was dismayed by the recent Egyptian-Jordanian statement limiting the scope of PLO representation to Palestinians living outside of Jordan. In order to slow down the U.S.-initiated diplomatic momentum, Moscow decided to bolster the international status of the PLO. For example, if the Soviet Union, as cosponsor of the Geneva Conference, openly insisted on PLO participation there, Egypt would find it difficult to attend without the PLO, whereas Israel would refuse to participate if it were present. If there were no conference, and no settlement, the United States would lose its leverage over the Arabs, thus enabling the Soviet Union to reestablish its influence in Egypt and Syria. The Soviets therefore issued a statement that expressed support for PLO participation in the Geneva Peace Conference with equal rights to the other participants.[122] The Soviet Union went further and undertook an initiative at the United Nations that, in September, led to the invitation to Yasir Arafat to address the General Assembly two months later. The Soviets enlisted the help of 100 nations to endorse the invitation.[123]

These achievements of the PLO in the international sphere, coupled with the United States' inability to effect a Jordanian-Israeli disengagement agreement, led Egypt to transfer its support from Jordan to the PLO. On September 21, President Sadat joined Hafiz al-Assad and Yasir Arafat in issuing a statement that designated the PLO as sole representative of all the Palestinians. This was a reversal of the policy statement he had issued with King Hussein in July. The international success of the PLO had become too important an asset to ignore, and its inclusion in the Arab diplomatic campaign seemed to promise great benefit. In addition, both Egypt and Syria had narrower ulterior motives for adopting a policy that removed Jordan from the diplomatic scene. Each, for internal political reasons, hoped that the United States would arrange a second separation-of-forces agreement between their respective armies and that of Israel, whereby they would retrieve more of the occupied territories. They viewed the deliberations over a disengagement between Jordan and Israel as merely an unwanted delay. While King Hussein was visiting Washington in August, Egyptian Foreign Minister Fahmi was also there lobbying to have a new Egyptian-Israeli agreement take precedence over all others.[124] Realizing that they could not achieve an interim Jordanian-

---

[122]*Al-Quds*, Aug. 4, 1974.
[123]Price, "Jordan and Palestinians," p. 8.
[124]Sheehan, "Step by Step," p. 46.

Israeli agreement without precipitating a crisis with Israel, the Americans shelved the idea in favor of the Egyptian proposal for keeping the Middle East negotiating process in motion.

THE RABAT CONFERENCE, 1974

The lingering contest between Jordan and the PLO was finally resolved at the 7th Arab Summit Conference, which was convened at Rabat, Morocco, one year after the Yom Kippur War (October 26–29, 1974). Officially, the summit had been convoked to draw up a united Arab political and military strategy for effecting an Israeli withdrawal from the occupied territories. The most important item on the agenda, however, was to decide upon the future representation of the Palestinians and the future responsibility for the West Bank. For the first time in the ten-year history of the Arab summit conferences, the PLO was invited to participate on an equal footing with the national delegations. This in itself was ample indication that the Arab heads of state were coming to Rabat in order to divest Jordan of its responsibility for the West Bank and to grant this responsibility to the PLO. Nonetheless, King Hussein attended the conference in order to expound his own views there.

In a thirty-three-page speech, delivered during a three-hour debate on October 27, the king asked the Arab heads of state to retract their unpublished decision, taken the previous year at the 6th Arab Summit held in Algeria, which recommended the recognition of the PLO as the sole legitimate representative of the Palestinian people. Although Jordan did not oppose considering the PLO the legitimate representative of the Palestinians, it could not agree to the title of *sole* representative. Who, then, would be responsible for the Palestinians in Jordan, two-thirds of the Jordanian population? The king's position revolved around four main points:

1. As Jordan did not consider Palestinian rights to be limited to the establishment of a Palestinian state in the West Bank, it wanted an official authorization from the Summit to coordinate its efforts with the other two confrontation states (Egypt and Syria).
2. When Israel withdrew from the West Bank, Jordan would undertake to allow UN forces to take the place of the Israeli forces on the condition that Jordanians and Palestinians participate together in the administration of the area on a basis of common understanding and reciprocity.

3. Jordan was prepared to arrange for a referendum in the area—with all the necessary guarantees and under international supervision—in which the Palestinians would be able to choose whether they wanted to set up a Palestinian state or be united with Jordan, either completely or federally.
4. If the Summit persisted in recognizing the PLO as the sole legitimate representative of the Palestinian people, Jordan would divest itself of any responsibility toward the Palestinian problem, and would refrain from participating in any international forum to discuss the problem.[125]

The Arab heads of state, however, were unimpressed: As the PLO was popular, its popularity had to be exploited in consolidating the political advantages that the Arabs had gained in the 1973 war. The resolution that they passed on October 29 thus stated that the PLO was the sole legitimate representative of the Palestinian people, and that it had the right to establish a "national authority" in the West Bank and the Gaza Strip. For several Arab leaders, this was an hour of sweet revenge against a king who for years had allowed himself to pursue independent policies contrary to public opinion in the Arab world. Houari Boumediene, the president of Algeria, expressed the prevailing sentiment to King Hussein's face in bitingly sarcastic words: "I would say that the role of the Hashimite regime ended with the battles of Ramadhan [the Yom Kippur War]; Jordan must therefore return to its own East Bank and leave the affairs of the Palestinians to the Palestinians."

Hussein's reaction, despite the humiliation, was dignified and restrained. He even pledged his country "to adopt the same national position as its brothers and carry out its duties to support, assist, back and cooperate, in order to enable the PLO to carry out its responsibilities and great burden." In justification of his own position, he maintained that the subject taken up by the summit had been inappropriate. Instead of discussing the means by which to liberate the occupied territories, the summit dwelled upon the question of who would rule them after their liberation. Jordan, the king stressed, had been motivated not by "any desire to impose a trusteeship on anyone" but by the belief that the Palestine problem belonged to the entire Arab nation—thus affecting the destiny of each member state—and was not merely the responsibility of any one state or organization.[126]

---

[125]*Keesings*, ME/4740/A, Oct. 28, 1974.
[126]Ibid., ME/4744/A, Nov. 1, 1974.

Despite his previous avowals that Jordan would divest itself of all responsibility toward the Palestine problem, the king undertook to continue to maintain material responsibilities and administrative services regarding the West Bank, until new arrangements in keeping with the changed situation could be made. He would also keep the bridges across the Jordan open to commerce and travel. Moreover, Jordan would remain the homeland of any Palestinian wishing to be one of its citizens, whereas those who opted for Palestinian citizenship (which did not exist) would enjoy the same rights in Jordan as did the citizens of other Arab states.

The king's position was not simply altruistic. The West Bank was greatly dependent on its connection with Jordan, a dependence that the regime utilized to retain influence there. Jordan was the West Bankers' lifeline to the Arab world. In order to travel abroad, West Bankers had to carry Jordanian passports. In order to study at Arab universities, West Bank students had to pass Jordanian matriculation exams. Jordanian consent to the maintenance of the "open bridges" enabled almost a million Arabs to pass yearly between the West Bank and the Arab world.

The West Bank's connection with Jordan was also an economic necessity. Agricultural exports from the West Bank over the "open bridges" totaled almost $100 million (£41 million) annually. In the West Bank, 6,000 to 10,000 former Jordanian civil servants continued to receive their salaries from Amman as part of what were called "perseverance funds" sent there to encourage nonacquiescence to Israeli rule. Public institutions, such as hospitals, schools, and homes for the aged, were also subsidized by Amman, which also made sizable contributions to the budget of the West Bank municipalities. To maintain these payments, even after the Rabat resolution, the summit itself awarded Jordan the sum of $250 million (£104 million).

Formally, whatever Jordan did subsequently in relation to the West Bank occurred in accordance with the Rabat decisions. In all his public pronouncements on the future of the West Bank, the king was careful to point out the ultimate responsibility of the PLO as the sole representative of Palestinian interests. On November 23, 1974, less than a month after the Rabat Conference, Hussein dissolved his parliament in which the West and East Banks had been represented on a 50-50 basis. The same day, Prime Minister Zayd al-Rifaʿi formed a new cabinet, dropping the number of Palestinian ministers from ten to four.

THE RETREAT FROM RABAT AND
THE TAMING OF THE PLO, 1976

Hussein's defeat at Rabat served to remind him once again that isolation in the Arab world could cost him dearly in his continual struggle with

Palestinian nationalism. He therefore set out to improve his relations with the other Arab leaders, a task now facilitated by his very acceptance of the Rabat resolutions, which officially put him in line with overall Arab policy and made him "clean." His major success was his rapprochement with Syria, a development expedited by the indirect negotiations that Egypt had begun with Israel in March 1975 over a second interim agreement.

Syria opposed the independent nature of Egypt's negotiation of agreements with Israel. The Arabs' strength, Syria felt, resided in united and coordinated action and a united strategy. Their weakness, as so often demonstrated in the past, lay in the individual pursuit of narrow national interests and advantages. Hence, the "small area" that Egypt would gain from a second agreement with Israel would be insignificant compared to the damage to the Arab cause that would result from Egypt's breaking of the ranks. Jordan, whose relations with Egypt had been cool since President Sadat resumed a pro-PLO policy the previous September also viewed Egypt's separate negotiations (which Sadat actually obtained by sabotaging the proposed Jordanian-Israeli disengagement plan)[127] as a symptom of abandonment by Cairo. Both Damascus and Amman concluded that Sadat was interested only in recovering Sinai, and that he was virtually uninterested in the fate of the Golan Heights and the West Bank. Moreover, whereas Egypt seemed to be recovering significant portions of its territory by negotiation, the inability of Syria and Jordan to do so apparently indicated that in order to retrieve their territories these two countries on Israel's eastern border might have to resort to war—or at least to the threat of war.[128]

In June 1975, President Hafiz al-Assad approached Jordan over the possibility of reconstructing a united Eastern Command, similar to the one that had existed (with Iraq's participation) until 1970. In order to pose a credible military threat to Israel, and in order to avoid the disadvantages that had led to Israel's victory over the Syrian army in 1973, Jordan's Arab Legion had to be properly utilized. Arab strategists were of the opinion that the absence of an active Jordanian front in the Yom Kippur War is what enabled Israel to mobilize the 10 brigades and 1,000 tanks and armored cars that drove the Syrian army back to within 40 kilometers of Damascus.[129] Had the 400-kilometer Jordanian-Israeli

---

[127]Sheehan, "Step by Step," p. 46.

[128]During a visit to Syria in May, Hussein accordingly proclaimed Jordan's willingness to fight Israel (*Haaretz*, May 15, 1975).

[129]Yehoshua Halamish, "The Revival of the Eastern Front," in *Yediot Aharonot* (Tel Aviv), July 7, 1975.

front been activated by Jordanian forces, and perhaps other Arab forces, they could have pinned down four to six Israeli brigades. In a future war with Israel, Jordan could play a role by protecting Syria's southern flank from Israeli ground and air attacks via northwest Jordan.

To fulfill these possible future roles, Jordan agreed to build fortifications along its northwestern front with Israel and to try to obtain U.S. Hawk ground-to-air missiles that, as an extension to Syria's own SAM-3 missile deployment, would provide an effective deterrent to Israeli air incursions from the south. Jordan would also seek to obtain U.S. fighter bombers that would grant it a surprise-attack capability against Israeli targets. Accordingly, in September 1975 King Hussein reiterated his May declaration that Jordan would participate if another war broke out between the Arabs and Israel. Later, in December, two Jordanian brigades took part in joint maneuvers with the Syrian army. In 1976, Jordan received twenty-four F-5 fighter-bombers from the United States and succeeded in negotiating for the receipt of sixteen batteries of Hawk missiles, which were paid for by Saudi Arabia.

The importance to Jordan of this Syrian connection was manifest in the socialist Ba'th party government's willingness to confer political legitimacy upon the pro-West monarchy, which Damascus had shortly before condemned as a reactionary regime. President Assad agreed not only to pay a state visit to Jordan in June 1975, but also to open negotiations for a political amalgamation of the two countries. On his arrival in Amman, Assad proclaimed that "Jordan and Syria are one nation, one state and one army."[130] For King Hussein, this acknowledgment from the PLO's most formidable supporter in the Arab world was a great step toward reintegrating Jordan into the diplomatic activity leading to the future Geneva Peace Conference. While steps toward political amalgamation were few—involving mainly the unification of certain laws in the personal domain—cooperation was initiated in the economic sphere, thereby adding credibility to the political rapprochement. This cooperation included the construction of a railway to run via Jordan from the Syrian port of Latakia to the oil-bearing area of eastern Arabia; the expansion of air communications between Damascus and Amman; the establishment of a free-trade zone on the Syrian-Jordanian border; the establishment of jointly owned transportation companies; and the joint construction of a new dam on the Yarmuk River.

---

[130]*Haaretz*, June 11, 1975.

Syria also derived political advantage from the rapprochement with Jordan. In March 1976, one year after a civil war had broken out in Lebanon between the Lebanese Christian communities on the one hand, and an alliance of the PLO and the leftist-oriented Muslims on the other, President Assad decided that Syria must intervene in this war unilaterally. His aim was to prevent the PLO and the Muslim left—who were backed primarily by Syria's enemy, Iraq—from gaining control of the country. If this were to happen, the diplomatic assault on the United States that President Assad was preparing in order to recover the Golan Heights would be impaired.[131] He feared that Iraq might use its influence on the PLO to get it to "heat up" the Lebanese-Israeli border, in order to involve Syria in clashes with Israel that would only reveal Syria's weakness. In addition, Israel might use this example of the Arabs' inability to restrain the PLO as an argument against surrendering the Golan to Syria. Despite Assad's intentions, however, he found himself deterred from intervening in the Lebanese civil war by the possibility that such intervention would lead to Israeli counterintervention.

To solve this problem, King Hussein came to President Assad's aid. While on a visit to Washington at the end of March 1976, the king pleaded Syria's case before the Ford administration.[132] Syria was entering Lebanon not to gain strategic advantages over Israel, he argued, but rather to contain the PLO and prevent the dismemberment of that country. In the long run, these objectives would be in Israel's interests, just as they were in the interest of peace. Hussein therefore asked his American hosts to persuade Israel to concur in the Syrian intervention. The king's arguments were apparently effective, for President Ford and Secretary of State Kissinger gave Syria the green light shortly thereafter. In April, the Syrian army entered Lebanon.

The Syrian intervention in Lebanon finally reversed a long tide of PLO successes that had followed upon the Rabat Conference. These successes, indeed, had begun less than a month after the conference, when, in November 1974, Yasir Arafat addressed the UN General Assembly. The Assembly then passed Resolution 3236, which recognized the PLO as the sole legitimate representative of the Palestinian people, advocated the participation of the PLO in all conferences dealing with a solution

---

[131]Avi-Dan, "The Syrian Involvement in the Lebanese Crisis," *Maarakhot* 251 (in Hebrew) (October 1976), pp. 25–26.

[132]*Haaretz*, March 31, 1976.

to the Middle East problem, and called for the realization of all Palestinian national rights. Shortly thereafter, France and other countries in the West joined the Eastern and Third World blocs in supporting the idea of a Palestinian state. In January 1976, the United States, which only two years before had communicated to Israel the understanding not to recognize the PLO until that organization stopped advocating Israel's destruction,[133] agreed to the participation of the PLO observer delegation in a UN Security Council debate over the West Bank.

Ironically, it was the sense of power that followed upon the PLO's achievements that impelled it to get more deeply involved in internal Lebanese politics. Many in the organization believed that by supporting the Muslim left in the civil war they could change the political balance in Lebanon, thereby weakening the Lebanese Christians who sought to curb fedayeen activity. Whereas Yasir Arafat allegedly opposed so deep an entanglement in Lebanese affairs, the more leftist organizations—the PFLP, the PDFLP, and the ALF (Arab Liberation Front)—felt an ideological commitment to the Lebanese left.[134] As in Jordan in 1970, Arafat conceded to the extremists rather than split the PLO or risk the loss of his leadership. The only difference was that in 1976 it was the Syrian army, rather than the Arab Legion, that broke the PLO's military strength. The toll of Palestinians who lost their lives in the conflict was reportedly over 23,000.[135]

On August 15, the PLO stronghold at Tell al-Zaatar near Beirut fell to the Christian forces attacking under cover of Syrian artillery. Following that and a chain of further Palestinian defeats, Saudi Arabia convoked a meeting of Arab leaders in the Saudi capital, Riyadh. The conference that convened in late October was attended by the heads of state of Saudi Arabia, Kuwait, Syria, Egypt, and Lebanon, and by the leader of the PLO, Yasir Arafat, all of whom arranged a truce in the Lebanese fighting.

The terms of this truce reflected a consensus among the participating Arab heads of state that the PLO was to blame for the Lebanese civil war. Accordingly, passages in the agreement clearly stipulated that the

---

[133]Golan, *Secret Conversations*, p. 127; see also, Jimmy Carter, *Keeping Faith: Memoirs of a President.* New York, 1982, p. 281.

[134]See Michael Hudson, "The Palestinian Factor in the Lebanese Civil War," *Middle East Journal* 32(3), 1978, pp. 261–278; see also, Dr. Yitzhak Ben-Gad, "The P.L.O. is Caught Up in a Hard and Painful Campaign—Against Its Own Will," in *Yediot Aharonot*, June 16, 1976.

[135]*New York Times*, Dec. 10, 1976.

Palestinian organization was to refrain from interfering in the internal affairs of all Arab countries, to respect the sovereignty of Lebanon, and to comply with the terms of the Cairo Agreement of 1969, which was supposed to regulate its activity there. The prevailing skepticism about Arafat's ability to exercise control over the PLO was manifest in the provision stating that henceforth the Cairo Agreement would be supervised by a commission composed of Egypt, Syria, Kuwait, and Saudi Arabia.

The greatest achievement of the Riyadh Conference, however, was the reconciliation effected between President Sadat of Egypt and President Assad of Syria, opening, it was thought, a new chapter in Arab diplomacy. At odds since the second Egyptian-Israeli Disengagement Agreement was negotiated in 1975, Egypt and Syria realized that they had to coordinate their diplomatic positions regarding Geneva in the light of new international factors. The following November, national elections in the United States would grant a new four-year mandate to the new president, thus enabling the administration to pursue more or less freely its desire to end the Middle East conflict. In order to exploit this opportunity to recover more of their lost territories, both Cairo and Damascus were determined to create conditions that would facilitate the convening of the Geneva Conference and to remove any obstacles that might impede it.

The main obstacle was the status granted to the PLO at Rabat that formally obligated the Arab states to insist on its participation at Geneva. However, as Israel refused to negotiate with the PLO, and as the PLO refused to adhere to UN Security Council Resolution 242 and continued to aim at setting up its "secular democratic state" in all of Palestine, it was difficult for the Arab states to convince the United States, as cosponsor of the conference, to invite the Palestinian organization. Therefore, at Riyadh in October, the rulers of Egypt, Syria, and Saudi Arabia made it clear to Arafat that they expected the PLO to change its line in demanding all of Palestine, and to begin talking about a Palestinian state in the West Bank and the Gaza Strip as a final objective. They also pressed Arafat to try to get the PLO to accept Resolution 242.[136]

This was not an easy task for the PLO leader. The Rejection Front within the organization (comprising the PFLP, the PFLP-GC, and the

---

[136]Ibid., Oct. 26, 1976 (Henry Tanner, "Decisive Turn About in Lebanon"); Dec. 10, 1976 (H. Tanner, "PLO, Set Back in Lebanon, Told by Allies to Compromise"); see also *Time*, Nov. 1, 1976.

ALF) still opposed PLO participation in a conference whose purposes were to arrive at a political settlement with Israel and to confer recognition upon the Jewish state within its May 1967 borders. As in 1970, the front still rejected the idea of changing the basic goals and strategy of the organization in order to help the Arab states obtain what these Palestinians considered transient and doubtful advantages that were only in their own national interests. Even Salah Khalaf, Arafat's own lieutenant in Fatah, was opposed to making any basic changes in the PLO's operation.[137] Consequently, despite the Arab pressures upon him, Arafat was again unwilling to risk losing his leadership or splitting the PLO and thus chose to defer the challenge. Accordingly, he postponed the thirteenth session of the Palestine National Congress that was scheduled to meet in Cairo in December 1976.

Egypt's reaction was not long in coming. If the PLO refused to make itself acceptable as a partner for negotiations over the West Bank, it did not matter. According to Resolution 242, Jordan was already a partner; indeed, if Jordan were to become responsible for recovering the West Bank, Israel might be more easily induced to discuss a withdrawal. In an interview with the *Washington Post* on December 30, 1976, President Sadat once again strayed from the principles of the Rabat Conference and proposed that any future Palestinian state in the West Bank and the Gaza Strip should be connected "institutionally" or "confederally" with Jordan. In mid-January 1977, while King Hussein was on an official visit in Aswan, Sadat went even further, explicitly declaring that Jordan had a role (albeit a limited one) to play at Geneva—namely, a role devoted to "withstanding Zionist aggression."[138] In order not to be accused of retreating from the Rabat resolutions, Sadat and Hussein worked out the following formula: Although both Jordan and the PLO would be at Geneva, Jordan would handle "matters of state" whereas the PLO would deal with all matters pertaining to Palestinian rights and the homeland. In January, President Assad also expressed his support for Sadat's ideas. In an interview with *Time* magazine on January 24, Assad declared: "If the P.L.O. refrains from participating at Geneva, this will not paralyze the movement of the Arab countries concerned. The Arab countries themselves will meet and decide what to do toward liberating occupied Arab territories and to ensure the rights of the Arab people of Palestine."

---

[137]*Haaretz,* Nov. 14, 1976.
[138]*Al-Quds,* Jan. 15, 1977.

In February 1977, when the new U.S. secretary of state, Cyrus Vance, visited the Middle East to explore the possibilities of convening the Geneva Conference during the following spring, both the Egyptian and Syrian presidents stressed their conviction that Jordan would exercise the dominant role in any future link with the Palestinians.[139] Assad, moreover, began to speak of an autonomous (rather than independent) Palestinian state, and Sadat went so far as to call for a Jordanian-Palestinian confederation even before Geneva, which meant that the PLO would be able to send delegates to the peace conference only as part of the Jordanian delegation.

But despite these pressures, the PLO was not as amenable as Egypt and Syria desired. Arafat, at Sadat's behest, swallowed his pride by sending a delegation to Amman in February 1977, and by holding a personal reconciliation with King Hussein in Cairo (their first meeting since 1970) one month later. Yet when the 13th Palestine National Congress was finally convened in Cairo in March, it gave the Arab leaders little satisfaction. Apparently wary lest Syria's and Egypt's eagerness to go to Geneva signaled their willingness to come to terms with Israel in exchange for the restoration of their territories—even at the expense of Palestinian interests—the PLO decided not to facilitate the reconvening of the peace conference by making itself acceptable for participation. Therefore, despite reports of concurrent pressure being applied by the major Arab states, the PLO did not delete passages from its charter calling for the destruction of Israel, nor did it accept Resolution 242. The only token concession it would make toward its Arab patrons was to refrain from making specific mention of the "Democratic Secular State" that it sought to establish in all of Palestine. In its place, however, came an ambiguous declaration of intention to liberate "all the occupied Arab lands" (article 9), without any indication of whether these were lands occupied in 1948 or 1967.[140]

The reference to the establishment of a state in the West Bank was even more ambiguous than it had been in 1974. The Congress merely reserved the "right to establish an independent national state upon its independent soil." The Congress also refused to commit itself to participating in the Geneva Conference, declaring only that it had a right to participate *independently* (i.e., not as part of a united Jordanian-Palestinian delegation, as suggested by Egypt) "in any international

---

[139]*Haaretz*, Feb. 22, 1977.
[140]See *al-Quds*, Mar. 21, 1977, for text of Congress resolutions.

forums, conferences, or efforts dealing with the Palestine problem or the Arab-Zionist conflict" (article 15). The Congress neither accepted Resolution 242 (article 1) nor changed its hostile policy toward Jordan, which—based on resolutions passed at its eighth and twelfth sessions (1971 and 1974)—called for the overthrow of the regime in Amman. This, in essence, constituted the PLO's emphatic rejection of President Sadat's call for a Jordanian-Palestinian link.

THE CONTEST FOR REPRESENTATION AT GENEVA

Between March and July 1977, there was relatively little diplomatic activity surrounding the convening of the Geneva Conference. Everyone was waiting to see the results of the general elections in Israel, held on May 17, and their aftermath. It was only after these elections and following the visit of the new prime minister, Menachem Begin, to the United States in July that the wheels of progress toward Geneva began to turn. The second visit of Cyrus Vance to the Middle East, in August, set them in full motion.

As Vance arrived in the Middle East, three factors formed the background to the talks that were to take place:

1. U.S. President Jimmy Carter, already in office for seven months, was depending on a diplomatic achievement in the Middle East to shore up his domestic prestige, which had dropped in the wake of unsuccessful domestic policies and a scandal involving his budget director. He therefore wished to convene the Geneva Conference at all costs.
2. The PLO, in refusing to adhere to Resolution 242, was still not eligible to attend the Geneva Conference.
3. Egypt and Syria were still officially bound by the Rabat resolutions to insist upon PLO participation in the conference.

Already guaranteed a role at Geneva, Jordan was waiting to see how these underlying factors would interact, for the outcome of this interaction would determine the extent of its own role.

An additional factor in the Vance mission was President Carter's genuine desire to have the PLO participate at Geneva. Carter viewed the Palestinian problem as falling at the heart of the Middle East conflict, a position that was influenced by a study conducted in 1975 at the American Brookings Institution in which Professor Zbigniew Brzezinski, who was to become Carter's national security adviser, participated.[141] The Brookings Report advocated self-determination for the Palestinians, to take the form of an independent Palestinian state or "a Palestinian entity voluntarily federated with Jordan." Two months after his inauguration, President Carter, speaking at Clinton, Massachusetts, went public with his support for a Palestinian "homeland"; still other administration statements at the time stressed the necessity of solving "the problem of the Palestinians."

By the time Cyrus Vance went to the Middle East in August 1977, the United States was determined to have the PLO participate in the Geneva Conference, and the president had already conveyed this message privately to Menachem Begin when the two met in Washington in July.[142] Still, the Carter administration could not insist on this participation, owing to the undertaking given to Israel by Henry Kissinger, at the time of the second Egypt-Israel Disengagement Agreement in 1975, that the United States would not recognize or negotiate with the PLO so long as the PLO did not recognize Israel's right to exist and did not accept UN Security Council Resolutions 242 and 338. If the impasse were to be broken, the Palestinian organization would have to be persuaded to accept these resolutions; this the administration sought to do by maintaining direct, if secret, contacts with Yasir Arafat, and by imploring the leaders of Syria, Egypt, and Saudi Arabia to exert their influence. If the PLO would yield in this regard, the Americans asserted, the United States would openly establish contacts with it and try to secure its invitation to Geneva.[143]

Moreover, in accepting the PLO's own claim that they rejected Resolution 242 because it ignored Palestinian national rights and referred only to "the problem of the refugees," President Carter, addressing the

---

[141]For a discussion of the degree to which the Brookings Report influenced Carter's thinking, see Zbigniew Brzezinski, *Peace and Principle: Memoirs of the National Security Adviser, 1977–1981.* London, 1983, pp. 84–86, 94, 102, 106; Cyrus Vance, *Hard Choices: Critical Years in America's Foreign Policy.* New York, 1983, pp. 163–164; see also Carter, *Keeping Faith,* pp. 276–277, for the president's personal views; cf. Bruce Maddy, "The Brookings Report and Carter Policy," *Leviathan* (Spring 1978), pp. 5–8.

[142]Vance, *Hard Choices,* p. 182.

[143]See Brzezinski, *Peace and Principle,* pp. 95, 105. In Saudi Arabia, Vance's spokesman declared that the United States no longer required the PLO to change passages in its National Charter (calling for the destruction of Israel) in order to qualify as a partner to the peace negotiations (*Haaretz,* Aug. 10, 1977).

press in Plains, Georgia, in August, let it be known that it was "O.K. with us" if the PLO conditioned its acceptance of the resolution on a declared proviso that "the Palestinians are not just refugees."[144] Indeed, Secretary Vance, in Saudi Arabia, went so far as to draft a proviso for the PLO: "The P.L.O. accepts United Nations Security Council Resolution 242, with the reservation that it considers that the resolution does not make adequate reference to the question of the Palestinians since it fails to make any reference to a homeland for the Palestinian people. It is recognized that the language of Resolution 242 relates to the right of all states in the Middle East to live in peace."[145] To encourage the PLO to accept this draft proviso, the president, at his press conference in Plains, publicly pledged that if it did, the United States would "reveal a tendency to recognize the PLO and support Palestinian efforts to establish a state of their own."

Secretary Vance's Arab hosts were less sanguine than he about having the PLO change its position. Despite the pressure that they themselves had exerted on the Palestinian organization when it was still smarting from its defeat in the Lebanese civil war, the 13th Palestine National Congress had refused that March to moderate the demands of its charter or to accept Resolution 242. Although the Americans preferred to ignore the PNC's basic intransigence, and to consider it a tactical ploy to improve the PLO's bargaining position,[146] the Arab heads of state were sure that the organization would remain ineligible for Geneva and thus have to be abandoned. Publicly, however, they had to continue to appear to be acting in the PLO's interests, so that the organization could not, as Hafiz al-Assad explained to Cyrus Vance, accuse them of "negotiating over its head." Thus, when Vance came to the Middle East in August, Syria suddenly announced that the PLO must participate at Geneva;[147]

---

[144]*Haaretz*, Aug. 9, 1977.

[145]Vance, *Hard Choices*, p. 188.

[146]The U.S. position is reflected in a study by the president of the American University of Beirut, Professor Malcolm Kerr, "America's Middle East Policy: Kissinger, Carter, and the Future," *Institute for Palestine Studies Papers*. No. 14, Beirut, 1980, p. 26. Referring to the PLO at its 13th National Congress, Kerr wrote: "The P.L.O. itself displayed eagerness to participate [in the Geneva negotiations], and some measure of readiness . . . to accommodate the United States' requirements in order to gain the latter's recognition." Such wishful thinking on the part of West Bank moderates was also evident, on the day following the Congress, in the headline: "P.L.O. to Participate in Any Peace Conference" (*al-Quds*, Mar. 21, 1977).

[147]*Haaretz*, Aug. 4 and Aug. 5, 1977.

its position earlier in the year had been that the organization's participation was not essential. Moreover, in the wake of Syria's apparent policy shift, Saudi Arabia, Egypt, and Jordan followed suit. Then, when Arafat—heartened by President Carter's readiness to ignore the "letter" of Resolution 242—made unscheduled visits to Damascus, Riyadh, and Cairo, these capitals suddenly began to promote the new idea of actually changing the resolution.

While Cyrus Vance was in Saudi Arabia, the Executive Council of the PLO met in Damascus and rejected the proviso for accepting Resolution 242, which the secretary of state himself had drafted. The PLO, it argued, would not accord recognition to the state of Israel in return for "a mere American offer to talk to it."[148] The Carter administration finally realized that the PLO could not be invited to the Geneva Peace Conference, at least for the time being. Accordingly, when the foreign ministers of Egypt, Syria, Jordan, and Israel came to the United States in September, in order to finalize arrangements for convening the conference, a way was sought to circumvent the Arabs' obligation to the PLO.

The Arab foreign ministers continued their ostensible insistence that a PLO delegation be invited to take its place at the conference table. In the face of Israeli objections, however, they proposed that PLO representatives be included in a joint Arab delegation. Israel's foreign minister, Moshe Dayan—who was negotiating via the Americans—refused to consider PLO delegates even in a joint delegation, but suggested that non-PLO Palestinian representatives (whom Israel would screen) be included in the Jordanian delegation. Egypt and Syria viewed this stance as too blatant an abandonment of the PLO, and Jordan objected to Dayan's suggestion, not wishing to be accused of trying to supersede the PLO's Rabat mandate.

Inadvertently or not, the United States found its way out of this impasse through a joint statement—issued, on October 1, with the other cochairman of the Geneva Conference, the Soviet Union—in which it recognized, for the first time, "legitimate Palestinian rights."[149] This was welcomed by the Arab foreign ministers, but more significantly, by the

---

[148]Vance, *Hard Choices,* p. 189; *Haaretz,* Aug. 29, 1977.

[149]Text appears in *New York Times,* Oct. 2, 1977. In February, Vance had coined the phrase, "legitimate Palestinian interests" (ibid., Feb. 12, 1977). For accounts of the negotiations just described, see Brzezinski, *Peace and Principle,* pp. 106–110; Vance, *Hard Choices,* pp. 191–194; Uzi Benziman, *Prime Minister Under Siege* (in Hebrew). Jerusalem, 1981, pp. 23–32.

PLO, who saw it as a vital asset in what it envisaged as its continuing, long-term struggle against Israel (now, as it believed, that it had successfully prevented the otherwise imminent Geneva Conference). However, after having given the Arab side considerable satisfaction, the Americans felt free to agree, by way of compensation to Israel, to Moshe Dayan's new proposal for a U.S.-Israel "working paper" that called for non-PLO Palestinians to be members of a joint Arab delegation at Geneva.[150]

Indeed, this is the plan Jordan had quietly been broaching with the Carter administration since February.[151] Therefore, it was a moment of satisfaction for King Hussein. The PLO was to be excluded from the expected Geneva Conference, whereas Jordan was to participate and to be responsible for the subject of West Bank borders—a giant step, in its eyes, toward assuming responsibility for the entire future of the West Bank.

---

[150]The U.S.-Israel working paper was made public on November 13 (*Haaretz,* Nov. 14, 1977). It constituted Israel's first concession to the idea that Palestinians, defined as such, were a party to any forthcoming negotiations.

[151]Vance, *Hard Choices,* p. 171.

FIVE

After the Sadat Peace Initiative

THE SADAT INITIATIVE AND THE ARAB REACTION

Jordan's advantage over the PLO in being delegated to represent the Palestinian interest in the Geneva Conference proved to be worthless, for within little more than a month, President Anwar al-Sadat embarked on a diplomatic initiative that nullified the Geneva framework. Since 1974, when the 12th Palestine National Congress refused to adhere to UN Resolution 242, Sadat had been entertaining the possibility of negotiating a final settlement with Israel without including the PLO. In 1977, this possibility became an imperative. In January of that year, when Sadat abolished government subsidies on Egypt's basic foodstuffs in an effort to raise funds for his nation's internal development, countrywide rioting nearly brought down his government. The episode revealed that these subsidies had kept 32 million people—80 percent of the Egyptian population—from starvation. At the same time, Egypt's military spending had already involved the country in a $7 billion (£2.9 billion) debt. Sadat's conclusion was that Egypt's reconstruction could no longer be delayed and that its funding would have to come at the expense of its military budget. In any case, reconstruction was possible only if Egypt's conflict with Israel were terminated.

The difficulties that had arisen in the summer of 1977 in connection with the Geneva Conference merely reinforced Sadat's developing desire to settle his conflict with Israel as quickly as possible, and on his own, if need be. In delaying a possible settlement with Israel, was he not subordinating the needs of 40 million Egyptians to the desires of some 3 million Palestinians, of the PLO, which professed to represent them, and of a handful of Arab leaders whom the PLO had intimidated into following its line? His conclusions were actually made before Egypt's foreign minister began discussing the peace conference in New York; for Sadat had already responded to Israeli overtures and sent his personal adviser, Muhammad Hassan al-Tuhami, to a secret meeting in Morocco with Moshe Dayan, the foreign minister in Menachem Begin's newly formed cabinet.[152] At the meeting, which took place on September 16 in Rabat, Dayan argued the improbability of attaining a peace settlement within the framework of Geneva. The Soviets, he stressed, were in no hurry to see the conflict resolved, and they would support the most extreme Arab demands in order to upstage the Americans. The Americans would then feel compelled to press Israel into making concessions that the latter might consider inimical to its security. This pattern would precipitate crises, and the talks would achieve nothing. Dayan suggested that Egypt and Israel settle their differences alone. In that way, he implied to Tuhami, Egypt would be able to recover Sinai without further ado.

The result of this meeting was soon publicly known. Addressing the Egyptian parliament on November 9, 1977, President Sadat, in what might have sounded like hyperbole, announced that he would even "go to the Knesset" in Jerusalem if that "would prevent the wounding of one of my soldiers, one of my officers." Within a few days, his "challenge" was taken up as Menachem Begin's government issued him an invitation to come to Jerusalem and address the Knesset, Israel's parliament. On November 19 the Egyptian president did come, arriving at Ben-Gurion Airport in a Misr-Air Egyptian Airline plane. Sadat was the first Arab head of state to set foot (publicly)[153] on Israeli soil since Israel's independence. He was received with an impressive display of warmth and dignity; thus a new stage of Middle Eastern diplomacy had gotten under way.

President Sadat's initiative, made independently of the other Arab states, reinforced the fear, entertained by Syria and Jordan since 1975, that Egypt might eventually desert them, leaving them to their own inferior resources to deal with Israel. The keystone of Arab strategy vis-à-vis Israel was united action, whether on the battlefield or at the negotiating table. In the years since the Arab oil boycott in 1973, Arab

---

[152]Benziman, *Prime Minister*, pp. 17–19.

[153]King Hussein was reported to have held secret meetings with Israeli leaders near Tel Aviv (see Note 77).

solidarity not only became stronger than it had ever been in the past, but it strengthened the Arab position in the diplomatic arena as well as in Western public opinion. To buttress their diplomatic stance, however, the Arabs had to be able to pose a credible military threat to Israel and, hence, to world peace. Here, the main role belonged to Egypt, given its vast manpower resources and its domination of Israel's western front; its exit from the Arab camp would automatically render any Arab military threat ineffective. Syria was thus unappeased even by Sadat's dramatic personal visit to Damascus prior to his Jerusalem journey, and it joined Libya, Algeria, and Southern Yemen in severing all relations with Egypt in early December. These states, together with the PLO, then formed a "Rejection Front," branding Sadat a traitor to the Arab cause and vowing to thwart his initiative.

JORDAN'S ATTITUDE TOWARD SADAT'S INITIATIVE

Jordan decided to pursue a more moderate course. On the one hand, it did not want to contribute to the breaking of the Arab camp, which, in itself, would jeopardize the chances of reconvening the Geneva Conference as well as its assured position in the peace process. King Hussein reportedly tried to mediate between Damascus and Cairo and stressed in all his public statements the need to preserve Arab solidarity. On the other hand, Hussein did not break with Sadat, preferring to wait and see what his initiative might produce. Certainly he could not ignore the fact that President Sadat had made no mention of the PLO when referring to the Palestinians in his Knesset speech or in subsequent pronouncements.

The public position that King Hussein evolved was characteristic of his talent for keeping all his options open. In order not to break with the Rejection Front, whose support he might need if Egypt's diplomacy left him in the lurch, he was careful not to identify with Sadat's initiative in either word or deed. On the other hand, in order to maintain the option of joining the initiative at some later date, he was careful not to condemn it as the Rejectionists had. Instead, his condemnations were reserved for what he called "Premier Begin's insufficient response to Sadat's generous offer of peace" and for the establishment of Jewish settlements in the West Bank, which, he claimed, demonstrated Israel's unwillingness to make peace. His only criticism of Sadat himself had to do with the Egyptian president's failure to plan his moves together with his "fellow Arab combatants of the 1967 War, to whom Egypt owes an obligation."[154]

All the same, Hussein was careful not to impugn the Egyptian president's *motives*. While visiting Cairo on December 8, for example, he asserted that Sadat's efforts were indeed "intended to achieve a just and lasting peace." On other occasions, the Hashimite king was wont to say that these efforts "might" contribute to peace. He also cited Egypt's sacrifices on behalf of the Arab cause—particularly that of the Palestinians—and publicly counseled his sister Arab states not to criticize Egypt too harshly. Another aspect of Jordan's stance was its minimization of the uniqueness of Sadat's venture, portraying it as "merely one more Arab initiative toward achieving peace." Jordan's initial reaction to the Jerusalem visit was to describe it as simply another step toward reconvening the Geneva Conference. The minister of information, Adnan Abu Awdah, applauded the visit for "breaking the ice and removing psychological barriers between Arabs and Israelis."[155]

In mid-December, however, Israel's proposals for a peace agreement with Egypt were presented by Premier Menachem Begin at a meeting with Anwar al-Sadat in the Egyptian city of Ismailia—and the proposals did not provide for the restoration of the West Bank to Jordan. In conversations during his visit to Jerusalem, Sadat had stipulated two conditions for concluding a separate peace with Israel: regaining all of Sinai and obtaining an arrangement concerning the occupied territories on Israel's eastern front that would enable him to claim that his initiative had advanced the Arab cause in general.

Regarding Sinai, the Israeli government had to decide if it could, indeed, return the entire peninsula (a possibility that Begin had intimated to Sadat) and, if so, according to which timetable. It was particularly difficult to surrender three strategic airfields—one at Refidim (Bir Gafgafah), the second just west of Eilat, and the third south of the Gaza Strip—as well as an Israeli civilian concentration of agricultural villages and the town of Yamit, also located just southwest of the Gaza Strip. All these installations had been set up by Israel's former minister of defense (1967–1974) himself, Moshe Dayan, and many in Israel deemed their retention vital to Israel's security.

As for the occupied territories on Israel's eastern front, Sadat apparently had asked Begin for a declaration that Israel was in principle willing to

---

[154]*Haaretz*, Dec. 2, 1977.
[155]Ibid., Nov. 24, 1977.

relinquish territory there in return for a peace agreement, without having to specify which areas would be relinquished.[156] In return, Israel could insist on a timetable for evacuating Sinai that would be consistent with its security needs. For the Begin government, however, permanent retention of the West Bank—which it began to call officially by its Biblical designation, Judea and Samaria—had a political significance more compelling than the continued retention of Israel's installations in Sinai. On ideological grounds, the prime minister's Likud party was pledged to the belief that all of Palestine west of the Jordan river was the natural homeland of the Jewish people; he therefore could not agree to relinquish authority over any of that land, not even in principle.[157]

Begin decided to offer Egypt the trade-off of Sinai for the West Bank: Israel would return all of Sinai to Egypt within five years of a peace agreement and would also grant the Arab residents of the West Bank and the Gaza Strip autonomy in all domains except security and foreign affairs, which would remain under Israel's control. Egypt, in its turn, would agree to suspend indefinitely a decision "on the question of sovereignty in these areas." The only provisions regarding Jordan were that the Arab residents of the autonomous area would be able to choose between Jordanian and Israeli citizenship, and that representatives of Jordan, together with those of Israel and the elected Administrative Council of the Autonomy, would decide upon the legislative framework of the Autonomy Plan and other "matters of common interest."[158]

The Begin proposals were not a proposition to which Jordan could accede. By explicitly precluding any Arab sovereignty in the West Bank and Gaza Strip, they deprived him of any reasonable justification for entering the peace negotiations. The Americans, who had given their qualified blessing to the proposals even before Begin presented them to the Egyptians, attempted to persuade the king to join the talks and try to change their terms.[159] Hussein, however, judged this probability too negligible for him to risk jeopardizing his relations with the other Arab states and his Palestinian subjects. Only if Israel had expressed its willingness to withdraw from parts, albeit unspecified, of the West Bank

---

[156]Oral communication from Mr. Shimon Peres (Dec. 31, 1978).

[157]Until 1967, Begin's party had also insisted that Transjordan be considered part of Mandated Palestine, never accepting its separation from "Cisjordan," by the British in 1922, nor the consequent prohibition on Jewish settlement there. The party was thus called the Revisionist party until 1948.

[158]*Haaretz*, Dec. 26, 1977.

[159]*Jerusalem Post*, Jan. 2, 1978.

could he have argued that his joining the negotiations might ultimately enable him to retrieve the entire West Bank, just as Egypt would recover the whole of Sinai. But were he to join under the conditions of the present proposals, he would, he feared, readily be branded a traitor.

Accordingly, the king condemned the Begin proposals as inflexible and insufficient. They were, he insisted, "not an opening position, but the limit of Israeli concessions." Hussein asserted that although he was in favor of peace, he would participate only in a broader peacemaking framework such as the Geneva Conference. He found no need, meanwhile, to attack President Sadat, for Sadat himself rejected the Begin proposals. On the contrary, when the Egyptian leader made a tour in January 1978 of European capitals to enlist support for his own position, the Jordanian monarch met with nine ambassadors, entreating their countries to extend to Sadat a sympathetic ear.[160]

FROM CAMP DAVID TO EGYPT'S PEACE WITH ISRAEL

Most of 1978 passed with few signs of progress in the Egyptian-Israeli negotiations—to the relief of the ruling circle in Jordan. By late summer, however, U.S. President Jimmy Carter, whose ineffectiveness in domestic affairs had been causing his ratings in the American public opinion polls to drop, became determined to move the peace negotiations forward under his own personal patronage—specifically, perhaps, in an effort to salvage his declining prestige. He invited Sadat and Begin and their top advisers to meet with him at the presidential retreat at Camp David, Maryland, to work out an accord while sheltered from the unsettling attention of the mass media. On September 22, after two weeks of intense haggling, the parties announced two framework agreements, one pertaining specifically to Egypt and the other to the West Bank and Gaza Strip.[161]

The essence of the Camp David agreements was that in return for accepting in principle Menachem Begin's proposal for Palestinian autonomy, President Sadat would receive several modifications to the original Autonomy Plan, together with Israel's undertaking to relinquish control of Sinai within three rather than five years (as originally proposed) of the signing of a peace treaty. The main modification in the Autonomy

---

[160]*Haaretz*, Feb. 6, 1978.
[161]Text appears in *Middle East Journal* 32(4), 1978, pp. 471–475.

Proposals was that autonomy was no longer to be seen as an indefinite solution, as Premier Begin had wished, but was herein limited to a five-year transitional period. In addition, instead of Israel being the sole authority for the establishment of the Autonomous Authority, this matter would be decided jointly by Israel, Egypt, and Jordan.

Jordan's role in the Autonomy Plan was further expanded from what it had been in the original proposals. Jordan would be a member of the committee that would decide on the final status of the West Bank and Gaza Strip at the end of five years; Jordanian citizens would serve in the police force in both of these areas; Jordanian soldiers would patrol the West Bank together with Israelis; and the negotiations for a peace treaty between Israel and Jordan would be based on the provisions and principles of UN Security Council Resolution 242, which provided for an Israeli withdrawal "from territories."

These concessions to Jordan, aimed at enticing it into joining the Egyptian-Israeli negotiations, came too late to achieve their purpose. The Camp David agreements, which dashed Arab hopes that the Egyptian-Israeli initiative would ultimately come to naught, provoked a strong reaction in the Arab world. The Rejection Front, consisting of Syria, Algeria, Libya, Southern Yemen, and the PLO, met in Damascus on September 23, 1978, and resolved to set up a unified military and political command to combat Anwar al-Sadat's policies; to seek a total severance of Arab economic, political, and cultural ties with Egypt; to seek a closer relationship between the Arab world and the Soviet Union in order to combat U.S. influence in the Middle East; and to seek the removal of the Arab League offices from Cairo. Reflecting the gravity with which the radical wing of the Arab world viewed the Camp David accords, Iraq and Syria even agreed to settle their bitter eight-year differences and to participate together in the 9th Arab Summit Conference, which was held in Baghdad on November 2. This conference, attended by all the Arab states except Egypt, expressed its contempt for the proposed autonomy by reaffirming its support for the PLO as the sole, legitimate representative of the Palestinians.

Although the Arab reaction to the Camp David accords and the terms of the accords pertaining to Jordan prevented Hussein from joining the Egyptian-Israeli peace talks, he was still unwilling to break with Egypt. He again sufficed himself by condemning Sadat's "diplomatic methods" and by rejecting the Camp David accords for violating Palestinian rights.[162]

---

[162]*Jerusalem Post*, Sept. 24, 1978.

But in view of the general anti-U.S. feeling among his Arab peers immediately after Camp David, he also felt it necessary to vindicate his special connection with the United States by asking the Americans to clarify their position on the future of East Jerusalem and Jewish settlements in the West Bank. The American reply, delivered by the assistant secretary of state for Middle Eastern affairs, Harold Saunders, should have satisfied King Hussein; he was told that the United States considered the Israeli annexation of East Jerusalem and the building of Jewish settlements in the West Bank to be illegal.[163]

But Hussein had already decided that it would be impolitic to adhere to the Camp David accords and that he would fight them instead. Even before Camp David, he had directed his supporters in the West Bank and the Gaza Strip to join ranks with pro-PLO elements and to obstruct any Israeli efforts to implement autonomy. To render credible his anti-autonomy intentions, the king decided to mend relations with the PLO, and on September 23 he received his erstwhile enemy, Yasir Arafat, in the company of Libya's ruler, Colonel Mu'ammar al-Qaddafi, in northern Jordan. In November two PLO delegations led by the chairman of the Palestine National Congress, Khalid al-Fahum, came to Amman to discuss ways in which his organization, together with Jordan, could combat the Autonomy Plan together. Three joint committees were set up to coordinate political activities, propaganda, and mobilization plans, respectively, for the residents of the West Bank and Gaza Strip in order to resist the Autonomy Plan. In October 1978 the PLO office in Amman was reactivated, and the king let it be known that he might allow the PLO to move explosives through Jordan to the West Bank.

However, Hussein's opposition to the Autonomy Plan provisions of the Camp David agreements did not prevent Egypt and Israel from finally signing a peace treaty on March 26, 1979. Jordan, in line with all the other Arab countries, reacted to this development by recalling its ambassador from Cairo and severing its diplomatic ties with Egypt. Hussein's lack of commitment had ended.

PREPARING AN ALTERNATIVE TO CAMP DAVID

What did not end with the signing of the Israel-Egypt peace treaty, however, was King Hussein's struggle with the PLO over the ultimate control of the West Bank and Gaza Strip. At most, the two veteran

---

[163]*Haaretz,* Oct. 25, 1978.

contenders agreed to join forces for the limited objective of thwarting the implementation of Israel's Autonomy Plan. The various factions of the PLO instructed their several partisans among the mayors and other leaders in the occupied territories to join the communists there in establishing the Committee for National Guidance, which began holding anti-autonomy rallies shortly after the signing of the Camp David agreements and prepared itself to coordinate further activities.[164] Jordan, for its part, informed its own partisans—such as the mayors of Bethlehem and Gaza, Elias Freij and Rashad al-Shawa; the former governor of Jerusalem, Anwar al-Khatib; the former Jordanian defense minister, Anwar Nuseibah; the former Jordanian member of parliament (MP), Hikmat al-Masri; and the leaders of the lawyers' and doctors' unions, Jiryis al-Khuri and Dr. Samih Katbah—that they should take emphatic public positions against the proposed autonomy, either within the Committee for National Guidance or independently.[165] By mobilizing all sections of the population, Jordan and the PLO believed they could convince their respective supporters in the West, as well as the Egyptians and Israelis, that they were indeed unrelenting in their opposition to the Autonomy Plan.

Nevertheless, any observer could note that on important issues the traditional animosities and suspicions remained. Jordan would not comply with PLO demands to rescind its ban on fedayeen operations from within Jordanian territory, nor did the PLO revoke the resolutions of the 8th and 12th Palestine National Congresses, which denied the legitimacy of the Hashimite regime in Jordan.

Ironically, it seemed at first that the main beneficiary of the Camp David accords was actually the PLO—both alone and in relation to Jordan. After losing the contest for representation at Geneva, and after being ignored in President Sadat's peace initiative, the Palestine Liberation Organization suddenly found itself in the political spotlight again. Prime Minister Begin had based his solution for the occupied territories on the Palestinians living there, rather than on Jordan; he had confirmed at Camp David that they had "legitimate rights"; and he had agreed to leave the future of the territories open to *later* discussion, thus inadvertently focusing attention on the PLO despite his own refusal to deal with it. The Palestinians in the occupied territories, together with the PLO, seized upon the inconsistencies in Begin's proposals and insisted

---

[164]Ibid., Oct. 17, 1978.
[165]Ibid., Oct. 25, 1978.

that his offer of autonomy was not commensurate with the "legitimate rights" that he had recognized. The "legitimate rights" of the Palestinians, they said, were a right to return to the lands they had left in 1948, a right to self-determination, and a right to national independence. Instead of waiting five years, they argued, an independent state should be established forthright. Moreover, since the Palestinians were guaranteed their "legitimate rights," Israel must deal with the PLO, which the Arab world and the United Nations had sanctioned as a representative of those rights.[166]

Menachem Begin, however, remained manifestly adamant in ignoring the PLO, reiterating his condemnation of the organization as "but a pack of killers" bent on the destruction of Israel. In Western Europe and the United States, however, Begin's position was met with increasing impatience by governments that identified the continuation of the world oil crisis with the continuation of Israeli occupation. In an effort to refute Begin's assertion that the PLO consisted of terrorists, Austria's chancellor, Bruno Kreisky, arranged to have Nobel peace prize winner, Willy Brandt, meet with Yasir Arafat in Vienna in July 1979. In September the U.S. ambassador to the United Nations, Andrew Young, in contradiction to his country's official policy, met with the PLO representative to the United Nations in New York. In Spain Arafat was accorded a state visit. In the following months, additional European governments received high-ranking delegations from the PLO, and in June 1980, the foreign ministers of the European Council, at a meeting in Venice, called for a PLO role in any peace negotiations.[167] This international success, accruing to the PLO without it having to accept UN Resolution 242 or to change its own charter or resolutions, encouraged the organization to anticipate mounting pressure on Israel to negotiate with it over an independent state.

Ironically, it was the PLO's optimistic appraisal of its own situation and its consequent continued refusal to recognize Israel even indirectly that nourished King Hussein's confidence that responsibility for the occupied territories must ultimately devolve upon him as the only realistic alternative to the Camp David process. When, therefore, the Egyptian-Israeli negotiations for a format for autonomy became bogged down during the summer of 1979, the king, in an interview with *Newsweek* magazine in early September, revived his United Arab Kingdom, or

---

[166]For example, see *al-Fajr*, (East Jerusalem), Sept. 19, 1978.
[167]Text appears in *Jerusalem Post*, June 15, 1980.

Federation, Plan of 1972, which provided for West Bank autonomy within Jordan.[168] Widely and bitterly condemned when first issued seven years previously, the king's plan was rejected neither by the Arab leaders with whom he privately broached the subject nor at the 10th Arab Summit Conference held in Tunis in November. The plan was not adopted due primarily to PLO opposition, but the fact that it was not publicly repudiated reflected the opinion then current in the Arab world that the United Arab Kingdom Plan might ultimately be the only way to prevent the occupied territories from being annexed by Israel.[169]

In order not to be accused of violating the mandate given to the PLO to be the "sole legitimate representative of the Palestinians" in 1974, the king remained careful to reiterate whenever possible his commitment to that principle. Nevertheless, in order to place the ultimate federation of the West and East Banks firmly under his own crown, he generally refrained, as in his speech before the UN General Assembly in December 1979, from any public advocacy of a Palestinian state; moreover, while always advocating the recognition of the Palestinians' legitimate rights, he defined these rights as "the right to a *national homeland*" and "the right to self-determination under conditions of total freedom."[170] This was the scenario that Hussein was wont to explain:

- When Israel implemented its total withdrawal from the occupied territories, Jordan—in its capacity as the recipient of those territories, under UN Security Council Resolution 242—would turn them over to the United Nations.
- The United Nations would then supervise a referendum in which, under conditions of total freedom, the Palestinians would exercise their right to self-determination, choosing whether to remain part of Jordan or to establish a Palestinian state.

In this way, King Hussein would delegate ultimate authority for determining their own future to the Palestinian residents of the occupied territories themselves, thereby denying the prerogative of "sole representative" to the PLO without being accused of usurping it for himself.

---

[168]*Haaretz*, Sept. 13, 1979.

[169]C. Legum, H. Shaked, D. Dishon (eds.), *Middle East Contemporary Survey, IV, 1979–1980* (hereafter *MECS*). New York, 1981, pp. 170–175.

[170]See, for example, the interview with Errol Rampersad in *International Herald Tribune* (Paris; special supplement on Jordan), December 1979.

However, the king was also not about to leave the final disposition of the occupied territories to chance. He would rather employ all the means at his disposal and take advantage of any opportunity that arose to enlist the allegiance of the local Arab population while, at the same time, seeking to limit the popularity and influence of the PLO. Experience had taught the king that the contest for the affection of the West Bank population, not to mention that of the Gaza Strip, was easier for the PLO than it was for the Hashimite regime. The PLO, with its clear-cut message of liberation and independence, and perhaps even social revolution, struck a natural chord with students and the ideologically inclined, commanding sentiments of identification and allegiance. Because these two elements of any population also tend to be the most vocal, especially in urban centers, one could hardly help feeling that PLO influence throughout the occupied territories was very pervasive. While countless rallies, demonstrations, and violent clashes with the Israeli authorities had often taken place in the name of the PLO, no such activity was recorded on behalf of Jordan. This is not to say that there were no individuals who favored the Hashimite regime over the PLO, but that their connection was practical rather than emotional. Their ranks comprised people interested in stability, conservatism, and prosperity—among them business men, farmers, religious functionaries, and civil servants, several of the latter having held positions in the Jordanian bureaucracy prior to 1967. One could add to this list those pragmatically minded people who perceived that should Israel ever release the occupied territories, it would only be to Jordan and certainly not to the PLO. However, because such people lacked either ideological or emotional commitment to Jordan, their opinions were low-key and often inaudible. The greatest manifestation of pro-Hashimite support could be felt on the two occasions when the image of PLO strength and its attendant promise were broken—after the PLO was expelled from Jordan in 1971 and after it was defeated in the Lebanese civil war of 1976. In both cases, however, the PLO eventually regained its previous popularity, largely because no "Jordanian option" materialized to end Israel's occupation.[171]

In 1979, King Hussein had no way of knowing when the PLO would again reach a nadir of popularity among the residents of the occupied territories, but he hoped that it would be when the world's powers and the Arab leaders finally decided to back his Federation Plan and to confer

---

[171]Bailey, "Changing Attitudes," pp. 161–164.

upon him the lead role in negotiating on behalf of the Palestinians. He also hoped that, when that occasion arose, he would be able to mobilize a majority of the population in the West Bank and the Gaza Strip in favor of his initiative.

As practical considerations were largely at the root of Hussein's potential following in the occupied territories, he found it necessary to control the flow of funds there. From 1967 to 1975, he had channeled annually to the West Bank about $50,000,000 (£20.8 million),[172] which supported religious and charitable institutions, subsidized municipal budgets, and payed the salaries of an estimated 6,000 to 10,000 former civil servants. Most of these monies were alloted to Jordan by the Khartoum Arab Summit Conference of 1967, and were paid by Saudi Arabia and, sometimes, by Kuwait and Libya. But after Rabat, when Jordan refused the PLO's demand for a say in the disposition of these funds, they were stopped, thus forcing King Hussein to cut back drastically on his payments, especially those directed to the municipalities. The PLO, early in 1978, found a way around the Jordanian obstacle through a "twin-cities" arrangement, whereby mayors from the occupied territories could obtain substantial grants from municipalities elsewhere in the Arab world, if the PLO would recommend them. The increase in influence that this arrangement promised to confer on the PLO immediately aroused Jordan's concern and prompted an intensive and successful diplomatic campaign by Jordan to guarantee that all such funds be deposited, pending payment, in the Arab Bank of Jordan.[173] As a release of the funds was subject to governmental permission according to law, the Jordanian government was again in a position to wield influence over the mayors who would personally have to come to Amman to request this release. As most of the mayors elected in 1976 had strong pro-PLO tendencies, these arrangements proved a significant victory for Jordan.

King Hussein scored another point in his battle with the PLO when, in November 1978, after the signing of the Camp David agreements, the Baghdad Summit Conference of Arab heads of state decided to set up a fund of $150 billion (£62.5 billion) to finance both the infrastructure

---

[172]Half the sum alloted to Jordan was designated for the West Bank (*MER, 1967*, p. 264; *MER, 1968*, p. 606).

[173]*MECS*, p. 285; another source for the financial and other forms of competition between the PLO and Jordan is Pinhas Inbari, *Triangle on the Jordan* (in Hebrew). Tel Aviv, 1982, pp. 94–97. Inbari was an Israel Radio reporter covering the West Bank.

of an independent Arab economy in the occupied territories as well as activities aimed at countering the Autonomy Plan. The fund was to be administered by a joint Jordan-PLO committee, which was indeed established in March 1979. Unlike the twin-cities arrangement, under which the PLO alone decided to whom monies would be allotted, Jordan henceforth was to share in the decision. Moreover, because the joint committee was to meet in Amman and because the funds at its disposal were to be deposited in Jordanian banks (and were therefore under the control of the Jordanian government), Jordan's influence over the disposal of the funds would be guaranteed. The main result of such an arrangement was that two-thirds of the 1980 allocation went to the Cooperative Societies for Agricultural Marketing, which, headed by one of Jordan's most consistent supporters, Tahsin al-Faris of Nablus, coordinated agricultural marketing for some 200 villages. Other beneficiaries were religious institutions, charitable societies, and institutions of higher learning, such as Najah College in Nablus and the Polytechnic Institute in Hebron. Organizations supportive of the PLO, such as the Committee for National Guidance, often found that funds were not forthcoming.

Despite its shortage of funds, however, the Committee for National Guidance was becoming a formidable factor in the political scene of the occupied territories. This was especially so in late 1979, after Israel had reversed its decision to expel the committee's most prominent figure, the mayor of Nablus, Bassam al-Shak'ah, owing largely to Shak'ah's own hunger strike and to widespread public disturbances organized by the committee. Concerned over this popularity, Jordan deemed it urgent to drive home the fact that it too was in the picture, according to the terms of Security Council Resolution 242. In January 1980, Jordan reopened its passport offices in several West Bank cities, transferring the authority for the issue and renewal of passports from the municipalities—most of whose mayors belonged to the Committee for National Guidance—to the Chambers of Commerce, which tended to be pro-Jordan.[174] To remind the West Bankers further that reality still tied them to Jordan—and not to the PLO—they were obliged to fill out forms requesting the renewal of their Jordanian citizenship; that, six years after the Rabat Summit Conference had made the PLO their "sole legitimate representative." In March the government decided that the Advisory Council, which had assumed the functions of Jordan's parliament a year after the Rabat Conference, would continue in operation "until conditions

---

[174]*MECS*, p. 284.

change"[175]—thus signifying that Jordan did not envisage holding elections for a new parliament without the participation of the West Bank. Finally, in June Jordan stressed its increasing level of concern for the West Bank and Gaza Strip by setting up a separate Ministry for Occupied Lands Affairs, which received the authority for releasing the funds that the Joint Committee had sanctioned.

On the diplomatic front, the king of Jordan urged an initiative that, while ostensibly promoting PLO participation in the peace process, was actually intended to preclude it. At the Arab Summit Conference in Tunis in November 1979, concurrent with his re-airing of the Federation Plan and in light of the faltering Israeli-Egyptian talks over autonomy, the king proposed the convocation of "a broader international peace conference," under the auspices of the United Nations, comprising the Arab states, the PLO, Western European states, the United States, and the Soviet Union.[176] The basis for discussion would be Resolutions 242 and 338. Hussein felt that his proposal would naturally attract the Soviet Union and Western Europe, given their consternation over what they considered a Pax-Americana, as embodied in the Camp David accords. He also hoped that the inclusion of the Soviet Union would oblige the Americans to deal more seriously with him than they had in the Camp David process, especially if they wished to broaden that peace process (which he felt would happen when the Autonomy Plan proved a failure), but without Moscow's participation. To make his flirtation with the Soviet Union more credible, Hussein even visited Moscow in 1980 and asked for Soviet arms. The inclusion of the PLO gave Hussein's proposal the necessary legitimacy in keeping with the Rabat resolutions, but by basing the discussions on UN Resolutions 242 and 338—which enjoyed international sanction—he in effect precluded PLO participation as, in the king's opinion, the PLO would never accept them.

King Hussein's effort was not in vain. As his was the major initiative proposed at the Tunis Conference, it was widely discussed and, although not officially adopted, it was, significantly, also not rejected. The king had further reason for satisfaction when the European Economic Community, meeting in Venice in June 1980, called for PLO participation in any negotiations discussing Middle East peace but stopped short of endorsing the idea of an independent Palestinian state. Here, as the king had anticipated, the PLO itself came to his aid; for when Fatah, Yasir

---

[175]*Keesings*, 30430 (Aug. 28, 1980).
[176]Inbari, *Triangle*, pp. 150–165.

Arafat's own, reputedly moderate, wing of the PLO, had held its general conference in Damascus in the previous month, it had explicitly rejected UN Resolutions 242 and 338.

In July 1980, King Hussein introduced his idea to Eastern Europe, where he also met with success. On a state visit to Rumania, the king managed to get President Nikolai Ceausescu's endorsement of a "broader international conference." Finally, in February 1981, Leonid Brezhnev, chairman of the Communist party of the Soviet Union, accorded his own blessing to the idea.

SHARON'S "PALESTINIAN JORDAN" SCHEME

After mid-1981, however, King Hussein's attention was distracted from his rivalry with the PLO by a new and perhaps more immediate threat—a threat not only to his future control over the West Bank but to his very survival in the East Bank as well. Elections held in Israel in June returned Menachem Begin to the premiership. The most dramatic change in Begin's new cabinet was the appointment of Ariel Sharon as minister of defense, an office that the prime minister himself had held since the resignation of Ezer Weizman in May 1980. Sharon, who had been serving as minister of agriculture, had, over the previous four years, devoted most of his energies to the establishment of some fifty-seven new Jewish settlements in the West Bank and Gaza Strip,[177] with the declared intention of ultimately annexing these areas to Israel.

Sharon had been adopting the position that Jordan, with its Palestinian majority, was already a de facto Palestinian state in every respect, except in terms of its monarchic Hashimite regime and its flag. He decried the fact that during "Black September" in 1970, Israel's threatened intervention had prevented Syria from aiding the PLO to topple the king. Had Israel not reinforced its army along Syria's border, at Washington's request, the PLO would have taken over Jordan, proclaimed a Palestinian state, and acquired a responsibility for maintaining the security and welfare of its new country. Such a development occurring now, according to Sharon, would restrain the current Palestinian leadership from encouraging the Palestinians in the occupied territories to demonstrate their opposition to Jewish settlement, and would change international opinion, which held the establishment of a Palestinian state in the

---

[177]Settlement Department, Jewish Agency (Jerusalem), *Map of Settlement in Eretz Israel*, March 1981.

occupied territories to be a necessity. It would therefore be in Israel's interest to facilitate a Palestinian take-over of Jordan whenever such an opportunity might arise.[178]

In November 1981, King Hussein came to Washington with the main purpose of obtaining a U.S. guarantee that Sharon's design would not come to fruition. The United States, which had been somewhat peeved with the king over the past two years in reaction to his attempts at obstructing the Autonomy Plan and to his proposals for Soviet participation in a new peace initiative, was nonetheless receptive to Hussein's concerns. Certainly the United States preferred a stable, moderate, pro-Western Hashimite kingdom as a northern neighbor to the oil-rich Arabian peninsula over a PLO-led state whose prospects for being unstable, extremist, and anti-Western were manifest. Moreover, Ronald Reagan, while campaigning for the presidency, had already envisaged a leading role for Jordan in "any final solution for the West Bank."[179] Therefore, perhaps after persuading the king to relinquish his advocacy of "a broader peace conference including the Soviet Union," President Reagan announced the United States' "commitment to the security and territorial integrity of Jordan." Perhaps, too, Ronald Reagan assured Hussein that the United States was itself giving serious consideration to a new initiative, one in which Jordan would indeed have a leading role. The king thus left Washington much relieved. Ironically, it turned out that Ariel Sharon's threat to remove the Hashimites from the Palestine scene was precisely what rendered them the most prominent feature of that scene.

---

[178]*Haaretz*, Sept. 3, 1982 (Matti Golan, "Who Invented Palestinian Jordan?"). The then foreign minister, Yitzhak Shamir, was also an advocate of Palestinian Jordan (see his "Camp David Remains the Only Direction," *Jerusalem Post*, Aug. 28, 1982).

[179]*Jerusalem Post*, Sept. 5, 1980.

SIX

In the Wake
of the Lebanon War:
The Reagan Proposals

PRESIDENT REAGAN IN SUPPORT OF JORDAN

It was Israel's invasion of Lebanon on June 6, 1982, that crystallized the United States' new ideas concerning Jordan. The invasion followed a ten-month truce between Israel and the PLO, a truce that sufficed to halt PLO attacks on Israel's northern border but also left the PLO's infrastructure in Lebanon intact and capable of mounting operations abroad. The two main features of that infrastructure were the virtual control of southern Lebanon, which was dotted with scores of PLO bases and positions, and the complete control of West Beirut, which served as the PLO capital and nerve-center of its worldwide activities, housing its various headquarters and facilities. Positioned in Lebanon were an estimated 20,000 PLO personnel bearing arms.

The year preceding the invasion was replete with rumors and indications that Israel was planning to invade Lebanon in order to destroy part or all of that infrastructure. The Israeli conception, identified primarily with Defense Minister Sharon, was that the eviction of the PLO from Lebanon, where it enjoyed an independent base of operation, would put an end to that organization and its influence. Deprived of its unfettered presence along the borders of Israel, the PLO would lose its role as a focus of hope for the Palestinians living in the occupied territories. Moreover, in having to operate under the scrutiny of other Arab governments, who would be careful not to let the PLO act in ways considered

109

detrimental to their own interests, the organization would lose much of its potential menace to the various leaders of the Arab world.

In the absence of PLO interference, the Arabs, Sharon apparently thought, would find it easier to acquiesce to Israel's gradual annexation of the occupied territories. As it was, he conceived, they had little other recourse. The Arab world was divided and weak at the time. Its leading power, Egypt, had made peace with Israel, and its second strongest state, Iraq, was bogged down in a war it had initiated with Iran. Diplomatically, as well, the Arab world did not present a united front, with Syria and Libya breaking up the Arab camp in their support for Iran against Arab Iraq. More significant was a worldwide oil glut, which had begun in 1981 and was now leading to a drop in Arab oil revenues and a decrease in Arab political influence. To top it all, the projected expulsion of the PLO from Lebanon would allow a Christian, Phalangist-led government to realign the country with the West—a realignment that, according to Sharon, would be to the United States' advantage, demonstrating to Washington that an activist Israel, looking after U.S. strategic interests in the Middle East, should be supported.

The invasion of Lebanon, ignited by a series of retaliatory actions after Israel's ambassador in London was shot by a breakaway PLO terrorist group in late May 1982, seemed to follow the scenario that Ariel Sharon had envisaged.[180] Within six days southern Lebanon was overrun, and within two weeks the Syrians were driven northward, their forces in the Bekaa Valley separated from those besieged in Beirut. On June 12, the Israeli army, already in East Beirut, set siege to the western side of the city—which was controlled by the PLO and the Syrians—and, through selective bombing and artillery shelling, sought to force the PLO to surrender. No country in the Arab world came to the defense of the PLO, and even Syria fought only when directly confronted by advancing Israeli forces. The United States, while often protesting vociferously against the shelling and bombing, did not take measures that could be effective in diverting Israel from its course.

American reactions to the Israeli invasion were mixed. Although undoubtedly satisfied over the potential return of U.S. influence to Lebanon, the Reagan administration was concerned that Jerusalem had

---

[180]Details of the war from Chaim Herzog, *The Arab-Israeli Wars.* New York, 1982, pp. 339–351. For the background of the war and the American attitudes to it, see Zeev Schiff, "Green Light, Lebanon," *Foreign Policy* 50 (Spring 1983), pp. 73–85.

failed to coordinate part, if not all, of its actions with Washington. It feared that Israeli success in an independent initiative of such magnitude would encourage Israel to believe that the United States, though a significant source of strength, was not a factor that needed to be taken into consideration in pursuing its own policies—and worse still, that Israel could pursue these policies with impunity, even if they proved detrimental to vital U.S. interests. For example, success in Lebanon might lead to Israel's annexation of the West Bank and could eventually also lead to an invasion of the East Bank and the replacement of the Hashimite regime with a Palestinian-led government, in keeping with Ariel Sharon's grand design.

To avert these possibilities, the Reagan administration adopted measures to neutralize Israel's gains from the invasion. One was to establish its patronage over the Lebanese government and encourage it to resist Israeli demands for a peace treaty and for wide extraterritorial security arrangements in southern Lebanon. Earlier in the war, it had been the United States that pressed Israel to accept a cease-fire with the PLO on June 12[181] and then immediately introduced its own mediation for the evacuation of the PLO and the Syrian army from Beirut. It was this mediation that enabled the United States to take credit for the evacuation of the Beirut-based PLO forces from Lebanon and their dispersion to six different countries, despite the fact that the U.S. effort had been facilitated by Israel's bombardment of West Beirut.

On the day in which this evacuation was completed—September 1, 1982—the United States took a further measure to check any Israeli aspirations that the war might have encouraged regarding the occupied territories. In an address to the nation to mark "the United States' success," President Reagan let it be known that he was favoring a solution to the Palestinian problem that required compromise and, hence, Israeli concessions.[182] The United States, in its capacity as a signatory to the Camp David agreements, would henceforth abandon its "neutral" position and begin expressing its own ideas. If, as was happening, Israel could advocate its annexation of the territories after the stipulated five-year period of autonomy, and if Egypt could advocate a Palestinian state, the United States now felt entitled to offer its own compromise: Palestinian autonomy in association with Jordan. The form that this "association"

---

[181]*Haaretz,* June 13, 1982.
[182]The complete text of the address may be found in *Jerusalem Post,* Sept. 3, 1982.

might take was left to negotiation, but an independent Palestinian state was explicitly ruled out. The Reagan Proposals, as they came to be known, provided for UN Security Council Resolution 242 to be the basis for a solution, together with the Camp David accords; for territorial changes to meet Israeli security needs; for a halt to Jewish settlement activities; and for Jerusalem to remain undivided, its future status also to be determined by negotiation. Jordan, the president hoped, would shortly join in the negotiation process.

The announcement of the Reagan Proposals coincided with what the Israeli government might otherwise have presented as an outright achievement—the completion of the PLO evacuation from Beirut—and immediately called Israel's war gains into question. The timing of the proposals, may, however, have been influenced even more by the visit to Washington in the previous week of Israel's defense minister, Ariel Sharon, who, unreservedly expounding his concept of "Jordan as the Palestinian State," heightened the fear among U.S. officials that he was indeed talking about short-range plans.[183] This is not to say that "the Jordanian option" suddenly surfaced as a result of the "Sharon design." U.S. policy planners had been giving this option consideration since as early as January 1978, when they realized that it was not only the most practicable option in light of the PLO refusal to accept Resolution 242, but also the option most favored by most of the Arab heads of state—even though they hesitated to say so in public.[184] However, now that the PLO and its influence in the Arab world were almost completely destroyed and the autonomy talks were in need of new direction, the Jordanian option presented itself as a natural alternative.

THE FEZ PEACE PLAN

The Reagan Proposals were but one reason for King Hussein to be heartened in the wake of the Lebanon War, which had witnessed the weakening, humiliation, and dispersion of the PLO in addition to its ensuing dependence on the Hashimite regime itself. As one of the six Arab countries to take in part of the PLO, Jordan gave refuge to over 500 Palestine Liberation Army troops[185] whose facilities and movements

---

[183]See ibid., Aug. 29, 1982 (Yosef Goell, "Sharon Spars in U.S. on Palestinians' Future").

[184]Carter, *Keeping Faith*, p. 302.

[185]*Al-Anwar*, Aug. 23, 1982. The Palestine Liberation Army consisted of regular units of the PLO, set up in 1965 and trained by Egypt, Syria, and Iraq.

he would henceforth control. Jordan had become important to Yasir Arafat as a counterweight and possible alternative to the heavy hand of Syria, which lay on several thousand other fedayeen of all the various groups. As a sign of Hussein's increased status in the Arab world, the 12th Arab Summit Conference, which met in Fez, Morocco, from September 8–10, chose him to head a seven-party delegation (Jordan, Saudi Arabia, Syria, Morocco, Algeria, Iraq, and the PLO) to the capitals of three permanent members of the Security Council (the Soviet Union, China, and France) to explain and try to enlist their support for the peace plan embodied in the Fez Resolutions.

The Fez Resolutions, or Peace Plan, adopted ten days after the announcement of the Reagan Proposals, differed from the latter in several significant respects.[186] The Fez Plan called for Israeli withdrawal from all the lands conquered in 1967, including Jerusalem; the dismantling of all the settlements established in the occupied territories; the granting of all rights to the Palestinians, led by the PLO, including "the right to return" (i.e., to their pre-1948 homes); the establishment of an independent Palestinian state, with Jerusalem as its capital; UN custodianship of the West Bank and the Gaza Strip (for a few months only); and UN Security Council guarantees for peace between all the states of the region, including the independent Palestinian state. The adoption of these proposals by all the Arab states (except Libya, which boycotted the conference, and Egypt, which was boycotted by it) and the PLO— as represented by Yasir Arafat—was considered to be a significant step toward a solution of the Arab-Israel dispute. The provision for a UN guarantee of peace for all the states of the region was taken to reflect the acceptance of Israel's existence by the Arab world. This in turn was understood by many in the West to be a result of the PLO's defeat in the Lebanon War.[187]

The adoption of these proposals in September 1982, however, was less a result of the Lebanon War than the result of a change that was introduced into the provision concerning peace—namely, that the Security Council would guarantee peace for all the states of the region (that is, if it could). Indeed, almost the identical proposals authored by King Fahd of Saudi Arabia had been rejected at the previous year's summit conference in Fez, because the provision concerning peace had confirmed

---

[186]Text appears in *al-Fajr*, Sept. 11, 1982.

[187]See, for example, *New York Times*, Sept. 12, 1982 (editorial and article by Henry Tanner, "Arab Moderates Offer New Proposals in New Unity").

"the *right* of the states of the region to live in peace."[188] Syria and Libya, in particular, had objected to giving Israel the *right* to peace; it implied not only the acceptance of Israel's existence but also the obligation to respect it. Once Israel's *right* to peace was dropped from the resolutions, however, even the PLO could accept them. According to PLO terminology, Israel was in the first place not a "state" (Arabic: *dawlah*), but rather a "Zionist entity" (*kiyān Ṣahyūnī*).[189] Second, as the West Bank and Gaza Strip were automatically to be relinquished to a temporary UN custodianship, the PLO was relieved of the necessity of negotiating with—and, by definition, recognizing—the Jewish state. Finally, as the provision for "an independent Palestinian state" did not limit that state to the West Bank and Gaza Strip, the PLO was still free to liberate the rest of Palestine in keeping with its "stages" plan, adopted at the 12th Palestine National Congress in 1974.

This reasoning notwithstanding, the adoption of the altered Fahd plan at Fez was seen in the West as an indication that the Arab world was ready to enter into negotiations with Israel. King Hussein, however, realized that the Fez Plan did not provide a realistic basis for bringing Israel into negotiations and was apparently less than enthusiastic in his presentation of the plan to the leaders of France, China, and the Soviet Union when he visited them as head of the Arab League delegation. Indeed, Yuri Andropov, the new chairman of the Communist party of the USSR, saw fit to warn the king of dire consequences should he dare adhere to the Reagan Proposals.[190]

Nevertheless, it was clear from his public statements that Hussein favored the Reagan Proposals. He referred to them as "a brave and courageous move" and "an important and historic moment that the Arabs should seize for making a serious bid for peace."[191] The overriding justification for his position, as frequently reiterated, was "the salvation of the land and its inhabitants before it was too late."[192] His reference was to the sixty-six new settlements established in the West Bank and Gaza Strip since 1977 by Menachem Begin's government and the twenty-

---

[188]Text appears in ibid., Oct. 6, 1981.

[189]See Harkabi, *Palestinians*, pp. 132 *et passim*.

[190]*Haaretz*, Dec. 5, 1982.

[191]See, for example, transcript of Hussein's television interviews with the BBC, Sept. 13, 1982 (*New York Times*, Sept. 15) and Nov. 4, 1982 (via *Jerusalem Post*, Nov. 7, 1982); see also *Jerusalem Post*, Dec. 24, 1982.

[192]See, for example, *Haaretz*, Feb. 7, 1983.

two more planned for the following two years.[193] As if to endorse the king's claims, a study published shortly afterward by a former Israeli deputy mayor of Jerusalem, Meron Benvenisti, highlighted the irreversible entanglement of Jewish and Arab villages and towns that was in progress everywhere in the occupied territories.[194]

Despite his support for the U.S. initiative, Hussein did not rush into any commitment to negotiate with Israel on the basis of the Reagan Proposals. Publicly, he made his adherence to the proposals contingent on three developments: (1) PLO agreement that he, and not the organization, would negotiate for the occupied territories, which was contrary to the exclusive PLO mandate granted at the Rabat Conference in 1974; (2) a freeze on Jewish settlement in the occupied territories effected by the United States; and (3) an Israeli withdrawal from Lebanon. The latter two conditions were intended as evidence that the United States could be relied upon to exert pressure on the Jewish state once negotiations got under way.[195] Privately, however, the king understood that in order to join the U.S. peace process he had to achieve three quite different measures. First, the PLO would have to eliminate itself as a realistic spokesman for the Palestinians. Second, he had to get support from a considerable section of the Arab world. Third, he had to receive an appeal from the population of the occupied territories to enter the peace process on their behalf.

ARAFAT STALLS ON THE REAGAN PROPOSALS

To get Yasir Arafat to disqualify himself, Hussein had to use the roundabout and seemingly paradoxical route of offering him a role in the peace process. Hussein did this when the two met in Amman in mid-October.[196] For Arafat or the PLO to play an active role in any negotiations, however, was really out of the question, because to negotiate with Israel they would have to recognize that country's existence (even if indirectly by accepting UN Resolution 242). This, in effect, would mean divesting the PLO of its very justification; the organization had been founded in 1964 specifically to destroy Israel ("to liberate Pales-

---

[193]Settlement Department, Jewish Agency (Jerusalem), *Map of Settlement in Eretz Israel,* Jul. 1982.

[194]See *Haaretz,* Nov. 12, 1982 (Amos Elon, "Ariel as a Symbol").

[195]*Maariv,* Nov. 12, 1982; *Jerusalem Post,* Jan. 6, 1983.

[196]*Haaretz,* Nov. 19, 1982.

tine"), as stated in its National Charter and as manifest in its many resolutions.

Recognition of Israel spelled destruction of the PLO for yet another reason: It would cause the PLO to split. Even if Arafat had been inclined to recognize Israel for tactical reasons, other leaders such as George Habash, Nayif Hawatmah, or Ahmad Jibril would reject such recognition, both on principle and as a binding precedent, and would quit the PLO in protest. Who would then speak for the Palestinian cause with authority or credibility? The answer, naturally, was: no one! The unity of the PLO therefore had to be maintained at all cost. Wishing to focus attention on this PLO problem as an obstacle to peace, King Hussein took advantage of several occasions to urge the PLO in public to recognize Israel "for the benefit of the Palestinian and Arab cause."[197]

Arafat was unable to accept for the PLO a silent role in any political process in which King Hussein would speak for the Palestinians, even if both sides coordinated their positions in advance. Even Hussein's offer of non-PLO Palestinian members in the Jordan delegation was unacceptable to Arafat.[198] To concede the role of chief negotiator to Hussein would be to forfeit perhaps the most important achievement of the PLO—the recognized right to be the sole, legitimate representative of the Palestinians. For that matter, what positions were worth coordinating with Jordan, when the Reagan Proposals specifically ignored the idea of an independent Palestinian state, leaving room only for Palestinian autonomy in a Hashimite federation of the East and West Banks? Such a federation was what King Hussein had already offered Yasir Arafat when the two first discussed the Reagan Proposals in October.

Under other circumstances, Arafat would have turned down these propositions without hesitation. In Autumn 1982, however, after the PLO had lost its independent base in Lebanon and after its defeat and expulsion from Beirut had demonstrated that it had little support in the Arab world, Arafat did not feel free to act purely on principle. Perceiving King Hussein's strengthened position and consequent self-confidence, he feared that an outright PLO rejection of the Reagan peace process would but facilitate the king's entry into negotiations alone. To avert this danger, he agreed to hold discussions with the king. Even if Hussein eventually accepted the Reagan Proposals, Arafat felt, contact

---

[197]On BBC-TV (via *Haaretz*, Feb. 7, 1983).
[198]Ibid., Jan. 11, 1983.

with the king might still leave him with some control over the content of the peace talks.

In addition, Arafat was loath to do anything that might precipitate a break with the regime, as Jordan might one day have to be the main base of the fedayeen—that is, if their presence in Syria, where the government was enforcing severe restrictions on their movements, became unbearable.[199] Arafat also had to consider the Palestine Liberation Army units already stationed in Jordan; they, too, were subject to limitations and even arrest. Arafat nevertheless asked permission to boost their ranks to 4,000, by drafting Jordanian Palestinians.[200]

Arafat's initial decision, then, was to enter into discussions with Hussein over the Reagan Proposals in an effort to delay their adoption. He could afford this delay as he did not accept Hussein's thesis that time was running out for the salvation of the occupied territories—that it was "a question, at most, of months." The PLO leader, moreover, considered neither the 70 or so Jewish settlements, with their population of over 25,000 persons, nor Israeli plans for future settlements to be a cause for haste. If the United States could effect the dismantling of 70 settlements in order to return the occupied territories to the Arabs, he thought, it could also effect the dismantling of 85 or 90. On the other hand, if the Americans were incapable of dismantling the settlements already in existence (and this was a matter of some doubt given the large Israeli investment and personal interest involved, as well as the difficulty encountered in vacating even fewer settlements in Sinai earlier that year), then there was definitely no reason to hurry. On the contrary, the United States might be more motivated to press Israel on the settlements if, after having its present initiative rejected, it received new signals from the Arabs and the PLO that they would be ready for peace— if only the settlement issue were solved. By then, the Arab camp might also be stronger.

Nevertheless, to prevent the PLO from losing its international popularity—perhaps its only gain from the Lebanon debacle—by precipitously turning its back on a peace proposal, especially one put forth by President Reagan, Arafat had to disguise his true intentions. One ploy was to dodge the main issues glibly. When asked about the U.S. initiative, for example, he replied, "We are willing to talk to the United States if

---

[199]See Eric Rouleau, "Undesireable Guests," *Le Monde* (via *Haaretz*, Nov. 24, 1982).

[200]*Al-Awdah* (East Jerusalem), Apr. 22, 1983, p. 11.

the United States is willing to talk to us—without preconditions"[201] (i.e., without the PLO accepting Resolution 242). When asked whether he would sign a confederation agreement with Hussein, he replied, "The Palestinians and Jordanians are united in their hearts. That is more important than all the words written on paper."[202] When asked whether the PLO would give Jordan a mandate to represent the Palestinians, he replied, "We will give the mandate to Saudi Arabia, and Saudi Arabia can decide whether or not to give it to Jordan."[203] Another device was to plead inability; Arafat could not recognize Israel because recognition was his "last card";[204] he could not grant Hussein a mandate because he "had no permission" and was "bound by the Palestine National Congress."[205] Arafat also evaded decisions by postponing them—until he knew "what the Arabs think of the Reagan initiative and what Reagan thinks of the Fez Plan,"[206] until he learned "the results of the Arab League delegation to the different capitals,"[207] until "the Palestine National Council decides."[208]

To a major extent, of course, Arafat was not a free agent. Even if he personally had no reservations about the Reagan Proposals, for example, he could not ignore the strong opposition to them among members of the radical wing of the PLO—especially among the leaders Habash, Hawatmah, and Jibril who even took exception to the seventh point of the Fez Plan, which provided for peace among the states of the region, guaranteed by the Security Council.[209] These leaders were angry enough with Arafat because of the contact he maintained with Jordan and sought with Egypt.[210] The PLO radicals had been opposed to any contact with the Hashimite regime since Black September and the expulsion of the PLO from Jordan in 1971. They even objected to the contacts that the PLO had maintained with Jordan as part of the Rejection Front of the Arab States' effort to thwart the Camp David agreements. Contact with the Hashimites meant conferring legitimacy upon them, whereas the

---

[201]*Haaretz*, Mar. 6, 1983.
[202]Ibid., Dec. 2, 1982.
[203]Ibid., Apr. 8, 1983.
[204]*Jerusalem Post*, Dec. 30, 1982; *Le Figaro*, Apr. 12, 1983.
[205]*Haaretz*, Feb. 1 and Mar. 31, 1983.
[206]*Jerusalem Post*, Dec. 30, 1982.
[207]*Haaretz*, Jan. 11, 1983.
[208]Ibid., Feb. 13, 1983.
[209]Ibid., Feb. 20, 1983 (statement by George Habash).
[210]Ibid., Jan. 24, 1983 (statement by Nayif Hawatmah).

radicals were convinced that the monarchy in Jordan would have to be eliminated even prior to the liberation of Palestine. From the perspective of the PLO radicals, Egypt was a flagrant traitor to the Arab and Palestinian causes and had to be boycotted until it repudiated the peace with Israel and the Camp David process. They rejected Arafat's contention that Egypt, once returned to the Arab fold, would be a boon to the Palestinian cause; moreover, they took exception to his tendency to reward President Sadat's successor, Husni Mubarak, for his political and diplomatic support of the Palestinians during the Lebanon War by maintaining contact with the Egyptian regime.[211]

The radicals demanded that the PLO stick to the principles of its national charter and its "stages" plan of 1974, and that it refuse to negotiate with Israel, in any case until the military balance of power shifted in the Arabs' favor.[212] Living in Syria and the Lebanese Bekaa valley, under the watchful eye of the Ba'th party regime of President Hafiz al-Assad, the radicals may have had no choice but to adopt the position that was desired by the Syrians themselves. But developments in Syria ultimately contributed to their conviction that they had chosen the correct path.

Up until January 1983, the possibility that Syria could still serve as a bastion for the Palestinian cause seemed quite remote. During the war, Syria's losses in armor, airplanes, and air defense were tremendous. Israel shot down eighty-six Syrian fighter planes and found a way to incapacitate and destroy the SAM-2, SAM-3, and SAM-6 ground-to-air missiles that had provided Syrian forces with air cover. Israel had stopped short of driving the Syrian forces from the Bekaa region in northeastern Lebanon, as it had from Beirut, but the Syrians' vulnerability to air strikes made it only a question of time before Damascus recalled its army—and with it the PLO forces stationed in the Bekaa.

In February, however, matters changed dramatically. The Soviet Union, having studied Syria's postwar strategic needs and seeking an opportunity to frustrate a Pax-Americana in Lebanon, decided to supply Syria with ultrasophisticated SAM-5 ground-to-air missiles as a way of giving Syria air-defense capability and, thus, a new active role in events. Without clear air superiority, Israel was unlikely to embark on widespread hostilities against Syria. Moreover, because Israel had been suffering since September from constant guerrilla attacks against its troops in Lebanon, and because

---

[211]Ibid., Feb. 16, 1983 (statement by Ahmad Jibril).
[212]Ibid., Feb. 4, 1983 (statement by George Habash).

the Israeli Kahan Commission report (on the Phalangist massacre of Palestinians in the Beirut refugee camps, Sabra and Shatilla, in September) recommended the dismissal of Defense Minister Ariel Sharon,[213] Israel's willingness to continue fighting in Lebanon was much diminished—especially as it no longer enjoyed overwhelming air superiority. In the minds of the PLO radicals, the following scenario emerged. Syria would not be driven out of Lebanon. As a result, PLO fedayeen would join Syrian troops to harass Israeli forces deployed in the Shouf mountains and elsewhere. When Israel retreated southward as a result of its constant losses, Syria would reintroduce the PLO into Beirut. Meanwhile, Israel would be bogged down in Lebanon as long as Syria remained there, and would undergo a decline in its fighting capacity as well as in its morale at home. Hence, for the radicals of the PLO there was reason for fresh hope.

THE 16TH PALESTINE NATIONAL CONGRESS

Armed with this hope, the radicals came to the 16th Palestine National Congress (PNC), which was held in Algiers from February 14–24, 1983. It was here that the major issues concerning the Reagan Proposals and future relations with Jordan were to be decided. However, for most of the 400 participants at the Congress, news of the resurgence of the Syrian position was less compelling than the memories of the Palestinian debacle in Lebanon—memories of the death and suffering; the destruction of the Ein Hilwe and Rashidiyya refugee camps; the thousands of Palestinian men in the Israeli detention camp at Ansar, in southern Lebanon; the bombardment of West Beirut; the expulsion of the PLO; and the massacre at Sabra and Shatilla. The policies that many felt had led to this debacle—rejectionism, noncompromise, extremist demands, and a dependence on violence—now appeared to have been wrongly conceived. It was for this reason that Yasir Arafat, whom many participants believed had been seeking a political compromise solution to the Palestine problem since the war, was warmly welcomed when the conference began. Moreover, the impatience that many Palestinians had felt in relation to Syria and the radical sections of the PLO led to the coining of a new slogan—"the independence of decision"—meaning that the PNC should

---

[213]Text appears in *Jerusalem Post*, Feb. 9, 1983.

adopt resolutions only in the Palestinian interest rather than in the interests of Syria or Libya, as represented by the radical factions.[214]

According to certain reports, Arafat, although unwilling to accept the Reagan Proposals, asked the Congress not to condemn them outright, to agree to a confederation (not a *federation*) with Jordan at some undetermined point in the future, and to allow King Hussein—alone!— to open negotiations with the United States.[215] In this way the PLO would keep open political channels, which might be useful when circumstances improved. However, the radicals, led by Ahmad Jabril, rebelled against accepting any "dictat" from Jordan, and insisted on condemning the Reagan Proposals for not recognizing the PLO, for denying an independent Palestinian state, and for "changing the Palestinian question from one of national rights to a problem of Jordanian-Israeli borders."[216]

Eight days of frenetic debate ensued, after which the wishes of Yasir Arafat—namely, that Reagan's plan be rejected but not condemned, and that the Fez Plan be endorsed—were incorporated into the final resolutions.[217] In categorically rejecting the Reagan Proposals, the Congress declared that

> they do not satisfy, in terms of procedure or content, the permanent national rights of the Palestinian people, denying them the right of return, the right of self-determination, the right to establish an independent state, and the rights of the P.L.O. as the sole, legitimate representative of the Palestinian people. They also conflict with the principles of international jurisprudence. The Palestine National Congress thus declares that it refuses to consider them as a sound basis for a just and lasting settlement of the Palestinian problem and the Arab-Zionist conflict.

In rejecting the idea of autonomy within a Jordanian-led confederation, the Congress resolved "to adhere to the rights of the Palestinian people comprising the right of return, the right to self-determination and *the right to establish an independent state* under the leadership of the P.L.O.— rights that have been confirmed by Resolutions of the United Nations.

---

[214]See the editorial entitled "The Independence of Palestinian Decision" in *al-Quds*, Feb. 13, 1983. On the other hand, the radicals' slogans were "A United Position" and "A United Consensus"; in other words, the PNC must not ignore the radical position and split the PLO (see *al-Fajr* and *al-Sha'b*, Feb. 14, 1983).

[215]*Haaretz*, Feb. 16, 1983.

[216]See ibid., Dec. 21, 1982, for a similar statement by Hawatmah.

[217]Full Arabic text appears in *al-Fajr*, Feb. 27, 1983.

The Congress also believes that any future relations with Jordan on a confederal basis should be between two independent states." In order to negate the ideological basis of Hussein's federation plan (i.e., a federation between *one* people on the two banks of the Jordan) the Congress acknowledged the existence of "a special relationship" not within one people, but expressly "between the *two* peoples."

In rejecting a role for Jordan in the peace talks, the Congress resolved "to reject any plans aiming to infringe upon the right of the P.L.O. to be the sole representative of the Palestinian people in any form, whether mandate, deputation, or participation in the right of representation." The Congress went so far as to challenge the right of Jordan to speak even on behalf of the Palestinians living in the East Bank, by affirming that "the P.L.O. is the sole, legitimate representative of the Palestinian people, *whether inside or outside the occupied territories.*"

Because the radicals in the PLO were finally satisfied that the Fez Plan "does not conflict with the necessities of the political program and the decisions of the National Congress," they allowed the Congress, in its resolutions, to consider it "the minimum for the political movement of the Arab States," but with the stipulation that it be supplemented by military action as required to change the balance of power in favor of "the struggle" and of Palestinian and Arab rights. The Congress, out of deference to the radicals, also called for a strengthening of relations with Syria, "with whom we have important strategic ties" and in view of its common border with Israel.

Throughout the Palestinian world, everyone expressed satisfaction with the resolutions of the 16th Palestine National Congress. The radicals were pleased that the Reagan Proposals had been rejected and that the acceptance of the Fez Plan left room for a military solution of the Arab-Israel conflict.[218] The moderates, on the other hand, saw in the confirmation of the Fez Plan the PLO's determination to seek a political solution to the conflict. Moreover, they believed that the Reagan Proposals were not really rejected, given that, in rejecting them, the Congress had not actually used the word reject. In Nablus, for example, the former Jordanian Member of Parliament (MP) Hikmat al-Masri, found that "the most important decision taken is the assurance of Palestinian-Jordanian cooperation on behalf of the interests of the Palestine problem, which we hope will be confirmed in the liberation of the West Bank and the

---

[218]See ibid., Feb. 23, 1983.

Gaza Strip by means of peaceful negotiations."[219] On the same day, the East Jerusalem daily, *al-Quds*, ran the headline: "National Congress decides to leave door open for discussion with Washington." This headline was based on nothing more than a statement by Salah Khalaf, Arafat's deputy, claiming that "we only rejected the negative points in the Reagan Plan."

ARAFAT BREAKS OFF NEGOTIATIONS

However, Yasir Arafat knew that the National Congress had rejected the Reagan Proposals, because it was he who had engineered the rejection. He also knew that if he avoided the use of the word *reject* in the rejection, he could create sufficient uncertainty to be able to drag out his "discussion" with King Hussein for an indefinite period. With this in view, he avoided for over a month coming to Amman to continue the discussion, going instead from one Arab capital to another trying to get the Arab heads of state, especially the Saudi king and the Iraqi president, to persuade King Hussein not to break off relations with the PLO despite its rejection of the Reagan Proposals, and not to accede to these proposals alone.[220] At the same time, to keep the bargaining facade up, Arafat had his team in Amman pose unrealistic demands on the Jordanians—for example, that they obtain written U.S. guarantees of a complete Israeli withdrawal from the occupied territories, and that they allow the PLO to set up its main headquarters in, and to operate from, Jordan.[221]

Finally, on March 31, the PLO leader came to Amman for five days, holding talks with the king and other members of the Jordanian government. On his departure, he took with him the draft texts of two points on which he and the king had allegedly agreed:[222]

1. Regarding the Reagan Proposals: "Based on the understanding that the Reagan initiative recognizes the legitimate rights of the Palestinian people, the two sides [to this agreement] have confirmed the need for negotiations between the concerned parties."
2. Regarding Jordanian-Palestinian relations: "In view of the relations characterized by unity [Arabic: *al-'alaqat al-wahdawiyyah*] that exist

---

[219]Interview in *al-Quds*, Feb. 24, 1983.

[220]*Al-Awdah*, April 22, 1983, pp. 10–13 ("What Was discussed in the Talks between Yasir Arafat and King Hussein?").

[221]Ibid.; see also *Jerusalem Post*, Apr. 6, 1983.

[222]Reported texts appear in *al-Awdah*, April 22, 1983, p. 11.

between Jordan and Palestine, the discrepancy between the Fez resolutions and the Reagan initiative will be resolved."

The texts themselves reflect the debate that must have ensued between the king and Arafat. For example, when Arafat insisted that he was bound by the resolutions of the 16th Palestine National Congress, which rejected Reagan's *plan,* the king suggested that they change the term and refer instead to the Reagan *initiative.* When Arafat protested that Reagan had ruled out an independent Palestinian state and ignored the right of self-determination and the "right of return," the king reminded him that Reagan did, nevertheless, refer to "the legitimate rights of the Palestinian people," which—through negotiation or international arbitration—could eventually be interpreted to include self-determination, an independent state, and the repatriation of the refugees. When Arafat rebelled at the exclusion of the PLO—the sole legitimate representative of the Palestinians—from the negotiations, the king assured him that, as Reagan had called for negotiations between "all those directly concerned," there was still room for PLO participation, but that this would be easier to achieve—even with American backing—once negotiations were under way, because of Israeli objections.

Finally, in order to circumvent the basic incompatibility between King Hussein's design of federating two "provinces" under his rule, as favored by the Reagan Proposals, and the PLO's demand for an independent state, as adopted by the Fez Resolutions, the king suggested that if they merely cited the unity of the "two peoples" (thereby conceding his "one people" principle to PLO terminology), they could at least imply that there was a basis for accommodation along the lines of President Reagan's conception. However, Arafat, who wished to strengthen his demand for an independent state, insisted that its projected name, Palestine, be used and that *unity* be replaced by the vaguer term: *relations characterized by unity.*

In the end, although the text gave more prominence to the Palestinian issue than to Jordan's interests, King Hussein achieved his main goal of keeping the Reagan initiative alive. Yasir Arafat, for his part, had managed to get through the Amman talks without a break in PLO-Jordanian relations, even though he had had to settle for statements that only vaguely implied the true PLO positions and that indeed disguised what had usually, as a matter of policy, been stated aggressively. On the other hand, he knew as he left Amman on April 5 that the last word still remained with the Central Committee of his Fatah organization, which had in the meantime convened in Kuwait and was awaiting his arrival.

The meetings in Kuwait were held under the threat made by Hussein that if the PLO did not endorse the Reagan Proposals as agreed with Arafat, he would hold a plebiscite and "go it alone."[223] While reawakening Yasir Arafat's initial fears, this threat was not sufficient to have him prevail upon the Fatah Central Committee to agree to the king's terms. According to statements made by members of the committee, it was apparent that the tendency to forge better relations with Syria and to stick to extreme positions was strong. Arafat was encouraged to follow this tendency because of Syria's improved military situation and because of the Saudi appraisal that Arab bargaining power vis-à-vis Washington might improve as time went on.[224] To avert Hussein's threat "to go it alone," Arafat called for the convocation of an emergency Arab summit conference, which, he hoped, would reaffirm the Fez Resolutions and establish a consensus that Jordan could not transgress; the Moroccan king, Hasan II, had already sent out invitations for an emergency summit the day Arafat came to Kuwait. On April 9, the PLO chief sent two of his top aides, Hani al-Hasan and Khalil al-Wazir, to Amman to present King Hussein with his answer. Undoubtedly, it was drafted in terms not unlike the quote appearing that morning in the Kuwaiti daily, *al-Watan*, in which Arafat said: "It is unthinkable after all the struggle, the blood, and the martyrs, that we would authorize anyone to represent us."

ARAB STATES—FOR AND AGAINST THE REAGAN PROPOSALS

Although King Hussein would have been pleased if the PLO had given him a mandate to enter negotiations for the future of the occupied territories, it is unlikely that he expected it; nor was he necessarily sorry that it had not been forthcoming. In his opinion, the PLO had maneuvered itself out of the only practicable peace plan in the Middle East, thereby leaving him as the main candidate to represent the Arab side. For that possibility to materialize, however, the king still needed two developments. First, the Arab states had to give him a mandate, and second, the residents of the occupied territories themselves had to manifest their

---

[223]*Jerusalem Post*, Apr. 8, 1983.
[224]Ibid., Mar. 31, 1983.

willingness that he negotiate on their behalf. In neither possibility, however, did King Hussein have much room for hope.

In a chronically divided Arab world composed of militarily weak countries, solidarity is considered an ideal to be pursued as the only guarantee of strength and expression of national will. Politically, solidarity means a consensus regarding various positions to be adhered to, as determined at forums such as the permanent Arab League or the occasional Arab summit conferences. Yet, although Arab governments are often wont to pursue their individual interests in violation of the Arab consensus, they generally attempt to hide or disguise their actions to avert the danger that might ensue if their people were to feel they were betraying Arab strength and the Arab causes that this strength was intended to serve. Accordingly, if the king of Jordan were to accede to the Reagan Proposals on his own, thereby openly violating the consensus established at the Summit Conferences of Rabat (regarding Palestinian representation) and Fez (regarding a Palestinian State) in 1974 and 1982, respectively, he would run the risk that his Palestinian subjects, whose allegiance he had painstakingly cultivated for years, might, as in the past, consider him a traitor.

Hussein therefore hoped to circumvent the prevailing consensus by receiving either the individual public endorsements of a clear majority of the important Arab states or a collective endorsement expressed at a new summit conference. During the six months between October and April in which he had conducted his dialogue with Yasir Arafat, the king's strongest endorsement came from Egypt under President Husni Mubarak. Egypt itself had broken the Rabat consensus by agreeing at Camp David to negotiate autonomy on behalf of the Palestinians (in total disregard of the PLO mandate) and desired now to broaden the peace process under American auspices. Thus, in addition to appealing repeatedly to the PLO to recognize Israel unilaterally and disavow the use of force, thus making itself eligible for participation in the peace process, Egypt prodded it toward reaching agreement with Jordan.[225]

In addressing the Egyptian parliament in February, for example, foreign Minister Kamal Hasan Ali said, "The need for joint Jordanian-Palestinian action is immediate; not to be postponed even for one week. While we sit waiting, Israel establishes settlements in order to swallow up the West Bank."[226]

---

[225]Ibid., Dec. 30, 1982.
[226]Ibid., Feb. 10, 1983.

A few days later, Ali wired the Palestine National Congress in Algiers, calling on it to help "tighten the noose around Israel to prevent it from swallowing up the Arab land. With no land," Ali stressed, "there will be no Palestine problem."[227] In March President Mubarak addressed the Summit Conference of Non-Aligned Nations in Delhi and omitted any mention of the PLO or of an independent Palestinian state, calling instead for the establishment of "a Palestinian *entity* in the West Bank and Gaza Strip, with the aid of the Arab States—*Jordan,* in particular."[228]

The Egyptian position, however, did not find a strong public echo among many Arab leaders; the only exceptions were Egypt's relatively insignificant allies, Sudan and Oman, and the heads of state of Tunisia and Morocco who for years had been advocating a political solution to the Palestine problem. More significant was the support tendered by formerly rejectionist Iraq, whose desire to retain Egyptian and U.S. aid in its war against Iran and whose dependence on Jordan's port at Aqaba for supplies of war material undoubtedly engendered support for the Reagan Proposals.[229]

The major disappointment came from Saudi Arabia, which both the United States and Jordan expected to endorse the Reagan Proposals, despite the fact that King Fahd himself had authored the rival Fez Plan and had impressed on U.S. leaders, including former President Carter, that his advocacy of the independent Palestinian state was sincere.[230] Fahd was also convinced that the Arabs could still improve their bargaining power vis-à-vis Israel if they restored their solidarity and spoke with one voice, and he feared that Jordan's joining the Reagan initiative would only deepen the divisions within the Arab world. At a more immediate level, the Saudi king could see how Syria's military rehabilitation was regenerating enthusiasm and self-confidence among the Palestinians, and he feared that his endorsement of the Reagan Proposals might ignite a bitter reaction among the Palestinians living in his own kingdom where they constituted, among other things, some 50 percent of the country's school teachers.[231] The Saudis therefore discouraged King Hussein all along and, at the end of March, sent to Amman their foreign minister, Sa'ud al-Feisel, together with the head of the political department of

---

[227]*Haaretz*, Feb. 15, 1983.

[228]*Jerusalem Post*, Mar. 10, 1983.

[229]Ibid., Jan. 9, 1983.

[230]Carter, *Keeping Faith*, p. 302.

[231]Nabil Badran, "The Means of Survival: Education and the Palestinian Community," *Journal of Palestine Studies* 9(4), 1980, pp. 66–67.

the PLO, Faruq al-Qadumi, to persuade King Hussein to maintain his contact with Arafat, despite the PLO's impending final rejection of the Reagan Proposals, and to redirect his energies toward pushing for U.S. acceptance of the Fez Plan.[232]

Above all, however, it was Syria that again demonstrated that, by keeping the PLO and its expectations alive, it had the power to sabotage any effort to solve the Palestinian problem if Jordan were to be the main party. Not only did Syria exercise control over the main PLO forces deployed in the Lebanese Bekaa, which it still occupied, but so long as it remained a confrontation state in conflict with Israel, the Palestinians could still hope eventually to subdue the Jewish state from across its borders. In 1976 Syria had demonstrated through its anti-PLO intervention in Lebanon, which led to the death of 20,000 Palestinians, that neither the organization nor its cause took priority over Syria's own interests. Moreover, its subsequent revival of the PLO after subduing it showed that Syria believed that the PLO could still serve its interests and its efforts to dislodge Israel from the Golan Heights. In 1983, accordingly, Syria was not about to forgo the instrument by means of which it could prevent any Arab accommodation with Israel, so long as its own problem of the Golan Heights remained unsolved. Publicly, Syria let it be known that it "would stop at nothing to prevent any Arab factor from embarking upon peace talks with Israel" and that it "was capable of restraining any new Sadat."[233] At the beginning of March, it threatened to concentrate its forces along its border with Jordan if Hussein decided "to go it alone";[234] moreover, to ensure that Arafat rejected the draft texts that he took with him to Kuwait at the beginning of April, the Syrians warned him that any diversion from the Palestine National Congress resolutions "would divest him of legitimacy."[235]

INDECISION IN THE OCCUPIED TERRITORIES

Even without a total Arab consensus in favor of his joining the peace process, King Hussein might still have been able "to go it alone" and

---

[232]*Al-Awdah*, Apr. 22, 1983, p. 11.

[233]*Haaretz*, Feb. 27, 1983.

[234]*Jerusalem Post*, Mar. 3, 1983.

[235]*Haaretz*, Apr. 8, 1983. In the following month, Syria's overall displeasure with Arafat took a concrete form as it supported, if not instigated, a rebellion in Fatah against his leadership. Under Syrian influence, too, the PFLP and PDFLP expressed support for the rebellion in October (*Jerusalem Post*, Oct. 21, 1983).

live with the results if he had received a specific call from a large section of the inhabitants of the occupied territories asking him to represent them. Supporters of a "Jordanian option" were not lacking there; indeed, they included the most widely read West Bank daily newspaper, *al-Quds*, which often expressed the impatience harbored by many of its readers toward the rejectionist attitudes of the Arab countries and the PLO (the PLO they felt, had given Israel time to colonize and eventually to annex the territories).[236] Another West Bank journal, *al-Bayadir al-Siyasi*, in polling residents of the occupied territories prior to the convening of the Palestine National Congress, found that 80 percent of the respondents were in favor of a Jordanian-Palestine dialogue, which they hoped would lead to an end of the occupation.[237] In November 1982, young intellectuals from various parts of the West Bank took the initiative in meeting with the Israeli Labor party leader, Shimon Peres, to discuss formats for a Jordanian option.[238]

A sense of urgency pervaded the territories, mainly due to Israel's intensive settlement policy. When the Palestine National Congress convened in Algiers in February, it received a telegram from the mayor of Gaza, Rashad al-Shawa, saying, "From the dying city of Gaza, surrounded by Jewish settlements, we send you our greetings. . . . There is no alternative to a Jordanian-Palestinian federal union. It is the only way to salvage what is left of our occupied land and our survival in it."[239] The mayor of Bethlehem, Elias Freij, also wired the Congress, warning that "there are only two months left to prevent a final Israeli takeover of the West Bank and Gaza Strip. . . . The Congress must adopt resolutions that will make it possible to defend the Arab identity and land of the occupied territories."[240]

---

[236]Random examples of such expression in *al-Quds'* editorials appeared when Egypt and Jordan accepted the Rogers Plan (July 30, 1970); on the eve of the Rabat Conference (Oct. 25, 1974); when Anwar Sadat proposed a Jordanian-Palestinian union (Dec. 31, 1976); on the eve of Cyrus Vance's mission to the Middle East (Aug. 5, 1977); when the PLO rejected Sadat's peace initiative (Nov. 27, 1977); when President Reagan made his peace proposals (Sept. 2, 1982); and when the Hussein-Arafat talks broke down (April 12, 1983). The car belonging to the editor of *al-Quds*, Muhammad Abu Zuluf, was blown up in January 1980.

[237]*Haaretz*, Feb. 13, 1983.

[238]*Maariv*, Nov. 12, 1982.

[239]*Haaretz*, Feb. 16, 1983.

[240]Ibid., Feb. 15, 1983.

On the same occasion a West Bank engineer, Adnan al-Hallaq, expressed these sentiments on the front page of *al-Quds*, in an open letter called "Observers from the Side":

> Every day we see with our own eyes a new *fait accompli* extending Israel's presence in the occupied territories. . . . [Therefore] we must clutch at the Reagan Plan and insist on its implementation. . . . The Reagan Plan is based on a Jordanian-Palestinian rapprochement which we from the occupied territories ask the Congress to support . . . in view of the common and united destiny, which is not an offspring of the moment or of a specific interest, but a phenomenon with deep roots that go back to before the establishment of Israel in 1948.
>
> If what is necessary to end the occupation is to authorize Jordan and the P.L.O. to try a peaceful solution, then let that not be an obstacle. For there is no difference between a Jordanian and a Palestinian. A sacred cause must not be bound by formalities. If this authorization solves the problem and ends the Israeli occupation, let's have the heart of the matter and leave aside the husk. And after we've come to the shores of peace, we'll settle our affairs within the confines of our own house.[241]

In spite of these feelings, fear of the PLO was sufficiently strong to deter public figures from extending an actual invitation to King Hussein to negotiate on their behalf; many remembered 1978, when several of their peers were assassinated for supporting the peace initiative of President Sadat. Thus, when Elias Freij tried to enlist 200 signatories to such a petition in January 1983, he failed.[242] Significantly, the PLO criticized his effort in no uncertain terms. Its main organ in the occupied territories, the West Bank daily *al-Fajr*, expressed the line that the PLO leadership had confirmed in Algiers: "The mayors in the occupied territories are municipal figures. They have no political role to play. The P.L.O. is the only address. Let no one try to limit the Palestinian problem to the residents of the occupied territories, for they are only one part of the Palestinian nation."[243]

Without either the backing of the Arab states or the invitation by the inhabitants of the West Bank, King Hussein, upon receiving Arafat's negative reply on April 9, could only announce that he would not enter

---

[241]*Al-Quds*, Feb. 14, 1983.

[242]Oral communication (Feb. 27, 1983) from Prof. Menahem Milson, director of Israel Civil Administration (West Bank) from 1981 to 1982.

[243]*Al-Fajr*, Feb. 28, 1983.

any peace negotiations "separately or on behalf of anyone else."[244] It was immediately clear, however, that the Jordanian king did not consider this the end of the road. He would continue his struggle to highlight for the Palestinians the contrast between his own urgent goal of "saving the land" and the PLO's long-range dream of bringing Israel to its knees. In his statement to the nation on April 10, Hussein explained that he had worked out with Arafat a joint position "capable of pursuing political action which, with Arab support, could take advantage of the available opportunity to liberate our people, land, and above all, Arab Jerusalem," but that Arafat, in Kuwait, had "decided on a new course of action that did not give priority to saving the land." Hussein's reaction was to say, "It is best left to the P.L.O. and the Palestinian people to choose their own ways and means for the salvation of themselves and their land, and for the realization of their declared aims in whatever manner they see fit."

The ball was back into the court of the West Bankers and the Gazans. If they wished to salvage their lands, they would have to resolve the question of representation themselves and thus turn to the king. If, on April 10, 1983, Hussein was confident that before long they would do so, it was because the World Zionist Congress, meeting in Jerusalem that day, announced its intention to establish fifty-seven new settlements over the next thirty years.[245] If, however, the king was not confident, it was the result of another news item that morning reporting that a leading PLO moderate, Issam Sartawi, had been assassinated by Palestinian extremists in Portugal. Although carried out far afield, Sartawi's assassination would suffice to remind the Arabs in the occupied territories just what price they might have to pay if they strayed from the PLO line.

---

[244]*Jerusalem Post*, Apr. 11, 1983.
[245]*Haaretz*, Apr. 10, 1983.

CONCLUSIONS

Legitimacy Above All Else

On learning that the Palestine National Congress in Algiers had rejected the Reagan Proposals, the *New York Times* editorial of February 24, 1983, urged King Hussein to "step forward," as he was the only one "who can still give moral weight and tangible meaning to Palestinian rights. By offering Israel peace and security, he might liberate a million Arabs from Israeli occupation and extricate himself from thirty-five years of fruitless conflict. After the P.L.O.'s default, no one could blame the King for being reluctant, or even afraid. Yet, in the Middle East today, heroism may be the last route to realism."

The *New York Times* was accurate in suggesting that Hussein was the only one who could still salvage Palestinian rights—or land. Yet, its conclusion missed the mark on two other points. It was not fear of the PLO that would restrain King Hussein from joining the peace process; nor would the possibility of terminating the conflict with Israel dominate his decision on whether to join or not. First, the PLO could do him and his regime no more harm than it had in the past; second, he had considerations of greater immediacy than his conflict with Israel. For Hussein to be "heroic" meant something quite different; it meant risking the alienation of his Palestinian subjects. If, for example, the results of his "heroism" proved displeasing to them, it might set back his family's thirty-five years of effort to win them over; it might even undo forever what had kept his monarchy intact. Palestinians constituted 60 percent of his population on the East Bank alone: If he were to obtain authority for the Arabs of the West Bank and Gaza Strip, they would then constitute 75 percent of his united kingdom. King Hussein was therefore not inclined to be rash, even if "heroism" might solve the problems of others. The fact that he was still reigning in 1983, and was even a candidate for a peace process on behalf of the Palestinians, was evidence that the caution he had learned to exercise throughout the years had paid off.

Almost no one in the 1950s could have foreseen this reality. To have thought at the time that the desert-based, inexperienced Hashimite "royal family" ruling an almost resourceless state and supported by a small soldiery of backward bedouin could survive the influx of a larger and more sophisticated population of uprooted, frustrated, and restive people who considered their hosts traitors was absurd in itself. But the conviction that these same Palestinians would one day feel that Jordan was their home, and that the Hashimites were a legitimate regime, belonged virtually to King Hussein alone. It was this vision and a determined sense of mission—as a descendant of the Muslim Prophet—that enabled the king to survive ever-lurking danger and so formidable a succession of trials and setbacks as had befallen him, what with the assassination of his grandfather, the years of Nasserism, the Nabulsi government and Abu Nuwwar coup d'état, the 1966 riots, the loss of the West Bank, the PLO state-within-a-state, the Rabat Conference resolutions, and the Camp David accords. It was indeed this vision, this sense of mission, that enabled him still to remain optimistic.

King Hussein's central asset in handling the Palestinian challenge in Jordan was that he saw it as a struggle not between the Hashimites and the Palestinians but between the Hashimites and Palestinian nationalism. He was struggling for the hearts of the Palestinians who lived in Jordan— a relentless struggle between reality, as represented by himself, and dreams, as represented by the nationalists. On the face of it, all the cards were stacked against Jordan when the struggle began. A new homeland with nothing to offer, ruled by a regime suspected of betraying the Palestine cause, was pitted against promises to reunite Palestine as an Arab country, to return the refugees to their land and homes, and to redress an injured pride. Palestinian nationalism spoke in the language of revered values appealing to a sense of justice and, increasingly, a quest for revenge. Palestinian nationalism would fight to the end, whereas the Hashimite regime would gladly end the conflict with Israel and get on with the integration of its Palestinian subjects and the annexation of the West Bank. If, as defined by the American political scientist Seymour Martin Lipset, "legitimacy involves the capacity of the system to engender and maintain the belief that the existing political institutions are the most appropriate ones for the society,"[246] then Jordan got off to a poor start with the Palestinian majority of its society.

Under the surface, however, forces for the legitimation of the new Jordanian context were at work from the very beginning. If, as Lipset points out, "it is important, when discontinuity takes place, that the status of conservative groups and symbols are not threatened," it is noteworthy that most of the influential Palestinian notables (who had not been associated with the mufti of Jerusalem) were immediately appointed to the senate, to cabinet posts, or to governorships[247] and that the election of several of their followers to the Chamber of Deputies was also arranged. Similarly, Palestinians whose influence derived from their former positions in the British Mandatory civil service, were immediately integrated into the upper echelons of the Jordanian bureaucracy. Hence, for all the Palestinians who came within the influence networks of these people, there was soon someone in the system whom they knew. Finally, the regime was careful to cultivate the Palestinian religious community, utilizing to its utmost the fact of the king's descent from the Muslim Prophet. Relations with the fundamentalist Muslim Brotherhood were always particularly close, and when other politicial parties were banned in 1957, the Brotherhood was allowed to function freely.[248]

In accordance with another Lipset prescription for legitimacy—which suggests that new, politically active groups should be given easy access to the *legitimate* political institutions in order to win their loyalty to the system—we find that many of the leading, and especially young, oppositionists (such as Anwar Nuseibah, Anwar al-Khatib, and Qadri Tuqan) were gradually coopted into the system, often as cabinet ministers or ambassadors. Hazim Nuseibah of Jerusalem served long terms as Jordan's ambassador to the United Nations. Moreover, the adaptation of these oppositionists to the system was facilitated by King Hussein's creation (again, in Lipset's terms) of conditions that serve "to moderate the intensity of partisan battle." Whenever possible, and often to the point of danger, Hussein avoided taking action that ran counter to

---

[246]Seymour Martin Lipset, *Political Man: the Social Bases of Politics.* New York, 1960 (paperback edition, 1963), pp. 65–71.

[247]For details on these appointments, see Bailey, *Participation,* pp. 93–108.

[248]See Jean-Pierre Peroncel-Hugoz, "Prosperity Under the Shadow of Growing Fundamentalism: Part I," *Le Monde* (via *Haaretz,* Jun. 25, 1981).

Palestinian sentiment. He always remembered to define his government's projects and objectives in terms of "mobilization and concentration for the sake of Palestine." Publicly, he identified with these aims and often, along with the representatives of Palestinian nationalism, went to the extreme of proclaiming, in his direst hours, "we are all fedayeen."

Perhaps the main factor aiding the regime in gaining legitimacy among the Palestinians was its effectiveness. Effectiveness, or performance, as defined by Lipset, is "the extent to which the system satisfies the basic functions of government as most of the population sees them." Most notable in this respect was the economic development of the country. Jordan in the early 1980s was a prosperous country with a 9 percent growth rate, an average $1,500 (£625) per capita income, and no unemployment.[249] Amman had become one of the important financial centers of the Arab world, one in which Palestinians, who constituted 80 percent of the capital's 1.2 million population, represented the hub of the economy. In business, industry, and government agencies, Palestinians often held the highest positions.[250] Much of this economic development was fortuitous: The Arab oil boom, for example, provided job opportunities and high prices for agricultural produce; the Lebanese civil war caused many foreign and Arab companies to relocate to Amman; and the Iraq-Iran war brought much activity to the port of Aqaba. Nevertheless, the various economic plans of the government, a liberal fiscal policy, and a judicious use of foreign aid for developing an infrastructure enabled Jordan to take advantage of these windfalls when they came. Palestinians, no less than others, benefitted from the boom, many of them building sumptuous homes in East Bank cities.[251] Public services also revealed the effectiveness of the regime; indeed, this was an area for which the king was praised by Palestinians as "having no equal among Arab rulers."[252] And not least, the stability that, after 1971, made Jordan's prosperity possible and differentiated it from many of its Arab neighbors was seen by Palestinians, as well as by Jordanians, as an important measure of government effectiveness—despite the fact that this stability was initially achieved by expelling the PLO from the country.

---

[249]Peroncel-Hugoz, "Prosperity Under the Shadow of Growing Fundamentalism: Part II," *Le Monde* (via *Haaretz,* Jun. 26, 1981); Henry Carr, "New Prosperity Is Creating Frenzy of Business Activity," *International Herald Tribune* (special supplement on Jordan), December 1979.

[250]Atallah Mansour, "Jordan: Arab Oasis," *Haaretz,* Apr. 5, 1977.

[251]Atallah Mansour, "Jordan: 18 Years Later," *Haaretz,* Mar. 24, 1977.

[252]*Al-Quds,* Feb. 11, 1977.

Owing to Jordan's development and prosperity, many Palestinians acquired an admiration for the monarchy and a stake in the stability it provided. As of mid-1983, however, the depth and permanence of the legitimacy thus achieved by the regime had not yet been put to the test. In the past, the degree either of Palestinian acquiescence in the Hashimite regime or of enthusiasm for Palestinian nationalism had been determined primarily by the absence or presence of a realistic chance that nationalist goals could be achieved. The highest levels of nationalist enthusiasm were reached during the years when Nasser ruled Egypt and the UAR; when a union of Egypt, Syria, and Iraq seemed imminent (in 1963); when the PLO and Fatah began to operate (in 1966); and when the PLO maintained its military presence in Jordan (between 1968 and Black September). Had the Hashimite regime not enjoyed superior armed force at any of these moments, it would have been overthrown in favor of a nationalist Jordanian-Palestinian government mandated to proceed with the liberation of Palestine.

As all these precedents took place before the great prosperity in Jordan, and as the regime has maintained tight restrictions on organized political activity for years, one cannot be certain as to what extent vested interests might, in the future, restrain Palestinians from endorsing a new and promising nationalist revival, which might come at the expense of the regime. One envisages elements of restraint, however, on recalling events of the past when Jordan's Palestinians had not yet acquired their present vested interests. In 1970–1971, having experienced three years of nationalist fervor on the PLO model, the Palestinian populace was sufficiently fed up with chaos to desire only stability and to allow the king ruthlessly to eliminate the PLO presence from Jordan. The aversion to instability must be even greater now, given that more is at stake.

On the face of it, therefore, King Hussein's vision seems to have been realized: His Palestinian subjects, aware that Israel will not readily be destroyed, have begun to look forward to a future in Jordan and have acknowledged that Hussein might be as good a ruler as they can get. Ultimately, however, the outcome of his vision will become clear only when the future of the territories is resolved—and this the king knows. If, for example, the absence of political progress leads to Israel's annexation of the territories, new tensions in Hussein's relations with the Palestinians might well arise. Should this occur, one possible scenario is that a large part, if not all, of the Arab world—for reasons of pride and the Arabs' inability to give up Jerusalem—would rebel and commence to fight, insisting that Jordan become their forward base. However, as destruction on the scale of recent events in Lebanon would almost certainly ensue from such a war, impelling the king to resist such a danger, what would the Palestinians on the East Bank do? Would their vested interests in property and stability lead them to support the king, thereby bringing about a Jordanian identity and divorcing themselves from Palestinians elsewhere? Or would lingering loyalty to Palestine and its cause compel them sufficiently to challenge the king, thereby risking their wealth in war and opposition?

However, joining the peace process and obtaining authority for the occupied territories do not guarantee that the Hashimite regime will remain legitimate. Although Jordan is considered the most liberal of the Arab states,[253] the West Bank and Gazan populations are accustomed to a relatively free press and other forms, albeit limited, of political expression under Israeli occupation; hence, they might not easily succumb to the restrictions practiced in the East Bank.[254] If the regime is consequently forced to repress them, what will be the reaction east of the Jordan? Would not these same residents of "Palestine" be likely, moreover, to express themselves along Palestinian nationalist lines, calling on their East Bank brethren to establish a "Greater Palestine" on both banks, instead of the United Arab Kingdom of Hussein?

This scenario assumes, however, that Jordan can indeed retrieve the occupied territories intact, a possibility that is very remote in 1984. Twenty-five thousand Israelis already live in over 70 settlements in the occupied territories, in addition to the 100,000 living in areas that were Jordanian East Jerusalem between 1948 and 1967. In other words, there are at least 25,000 Jewish families—with material and, in some cases, ideological interests in the territories—who will not agree to relocate willingly or cheaply, if at all. To attempt to move most of these people out of their homes would not only be an act of great political risk to any Israeli cabinet, but such an action might, if pursued, ignite a civil war. A drastic reduction in the Israeli presence in the territories is thus not a measure an Israeli government would agree to; nor would a U.S. government press for this outcome. The United States would hardly wish to see the resultant chaos in the Middle East, as a civil war in Israel offers a temptation for Arab armies to enter the fray.

---

[253]Atallah Mansour, "Hussein Awaiting the Right Moment," *Haaretz,* Apr. 14, 1977; see also John Harbo, "The Palestinians—A Well-Educated Elite," *Aftenposten* (Oslo), Nov. 2, 1982.

[254]For West Bank attitudes toward political restrictions in Jordan, see "A Call . . . for Civil Liberties in Jordan," *al-Fajr,* Sept. 17, 1978.

Assuming, therefore, that a reduced "homeland" is all that King Hussein can ultimately reclaim, will the Palestinians there be grateful, or will they lay the blame on him? Even a clear mandate from them, in advance, might not eliminate the risk. Yet, such a mandate is essential if Hussein hopes, at all, to weather the expected storm.

Ironically, this very predicament may be to the Hashimites' advantage. The pattern of Israeli settlement and Israel's perceived security needs in the Jordan valley do indeed leave for future Arab sovereignty only patches of contiguous Arab habitation. One conceivable arrangement, therefore, might be to designate these patches, some eight or ten in number, as enclaves—autonomous enclaves belonging to Jordan but separated from the East Bank, just as Berlin is separated from West Germany. Under this arrangement, neither Israel nor the Arabs would be getting as much land as they want, and some fifteen Israeli settlements would be dismantled. Each party, however, would derive some benefit. The Palestinians would be governed by Arabs rather than by Jews, and they would be guaranteed that Israel would acquire no land in the enclaves. Israel would be afforded maximum security, owing primarily to its control of the areas surrounding the enclaves. In addition, the danger of an irredentist Palestinian nationalism emerging in the relinquished territories would be eliminated by their mutual separation; relations between each enclave and the East Bank would henceforth take precedence over the pattern of relations that had hitherto prevailed. Finally, as the continued security of the enclaves themselves would largely be determined by the nature of relations between Jordan and Israel, the Hashimite regime would benefit by attaining a domestic consensus against Palestinian nationalist, or other revolutionary, movements that sought to change the regime and, perhaps, combat Israel. Such security, in turn, would allow for more political freedom inside Jordan, and would lead eventually to a larger share of Palestinians in the decisionmaking bodies of their country.

From a Palestinian point of view, what they could salvage in 1983 was a far cry from what they could have gotten had the Palestinian nationalists been willing to compromise at any time in the past, beginning with the first partition plan (of Lord Peel) in 1937. Major opportunities were missed in 1947, 1967, and 1977. The Hashimites knew this all along and were willing to compromise. They could not do so, however, for the Palestinians were under the spell of nationalist leaders who considered any compromise with Zionism or the state of Israel to be treason. In mid-1984, thirty-six years after the establishment of Israel, most of the inhabitants of the occupied territories are still unable to decide whether to compromise, together with Hussein, and thus save their land, or to "stand firm" together with the PLO and bet on the millennia. However, unless they decide to be realistic, and unless they have the courage to ask the king explicitly to negotiate on their behalf, Hussein, himself, is not likely to be "heroic."

Index